GLOUCESTERSHIRE RAILWAYS

COLIN G. MAGGS

HALSGROVE

First published in Great Britain in 2010

British Library Cataloguing-in-Publication Data
A CIP record for this title is available from the British Library

ISBN 978 1 84114 913 4

HALSGROVE
Halsgrove House,
Ryelands Industrial Estate,
Bagley Road, Wellington, Somerset TA21 9PZ
Tel: 01823 653777   Fax: 01823 216796
email: sales@halsgrove.com

Part of the Halsgrove group of companies
Information on all Halsgrove titles is available at: www.halsgrove.com

Printed and bound in Great Britain by SRP, Exeter

This book is dedicated to
Colin Roberts in friendship

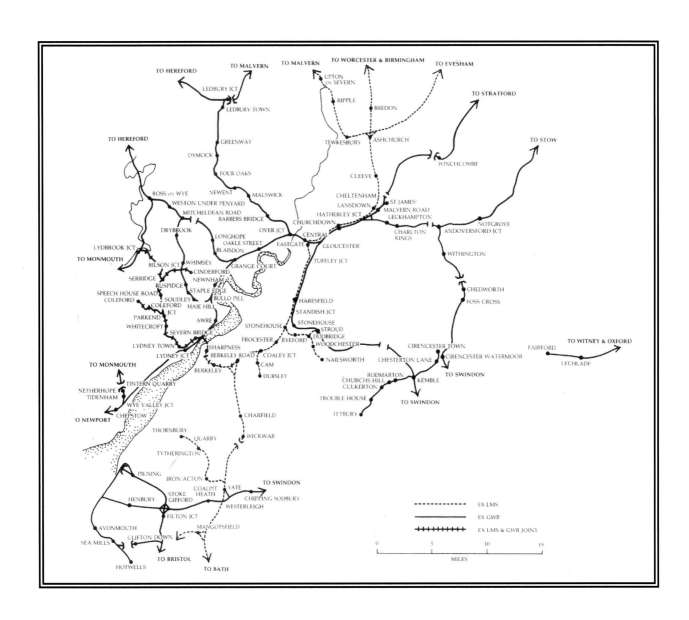

Contents

1 An Outline Survey of Railways in Gloucestershire

GLOUCESTERSHIRE HAS been sorely overlooked as a county with important railway features: there was a dense network of early railways in the Forest of Dean; the Bristol & Gloucestershire/Avon & Gloucestershire Railway which had a steam locomotive as early as 1835; another early line was the Cheltenham & Gloucester Tramway, while the 4,162yd Severn Bridge was the longest in England; additionally there were three major railway tunnels: the Severn, Sodbury and Sapperton.

At first the railway map of Gloucestershire seems complicated, but in

essence consists of two main companies: the Great Western Railway (GWR) and the Midland Railway (MR). The former ran through the Cotswolds on the southern border of the county and had lines radiating from Gloucester and Cheltenham. The Midland Railway ran north to south through the county sending branches into valleys of the south Cotswolds. In addition to these two principal companies, the Midland & South Western Junction Railway (MSWJR) as part of its route from Cheltenham to Southampton, ran from Andoversford to Cirencester. The Severn & Wye Joint Railway ran from Berkeley Road, on the MR's Gloucester to Bristol line, across the Severn Bridge to a maze of lines in the Forest of Dean.

Rationalisation in the nineteen-fifties and sixties saw most of the branch lines in the county closed, leaving just the two ex-GWR main lines to South Wales via Gloucester or the Severn Tunnel, and the former MR main line through Cheltenham and Gloucester to Bristol. Fortunately the county is blessed with three preserved railways: the Avon Valley Railway centred on Bitton; the Forest of Dean Railway and the Gloucestershire Warwickshire Railway.

The county was involved in the railway gauge question. The GWR and the Bristol & Gloucester Railway favoured the broad gauge of 7ft 0¼ in, whereas the MR preferred the standard gauge of 4ft 8½ in. Having two gauges prevented through running of rolling stock and thus created problems at stations such as Gloucester where the two gauges met. Eventually the cost and inconvenience of transhipment at the break of gauge caused the broad gauge lines to be converted.

As the rather complicated history of railways in Bristol and the Forest of Dean have been adequately recorded elsewhere – see 'Suggested Further Reading' – these areas have been omitted from this book.

Handbill advertising Weekly Runabout tickets, April 1954.

2 How a Railway was Created

IN THE nineteenth century, businessmen and landowners wishing to improve trade, increase the value of their property and invest their cash profitably, might propose a scheme for linking two places by a railway. The way they went about such a scheme followed a general pattern which can be described once and serve to tell the story of the creation of almost any railway in Gloucestershire. Several meetings would be called in the locality and provided that sufficient financial support was promised, a bill would be placed before Parliament, itself often proving an expensive process. Committees of the houses of Commons and Lords received evidence for and against the proposed line. If both houses passed the bill it became an Act of Parliament and the promoting company was then legally entitled to raise a stipulated sum of money to purchase land and build the railway between the two chosen places. Before going to Parliament a surveyor would have drawn plans. Ideally, a line would be straight, level, and pass through or close to chief settlements, yet using cheaper, rather than expensive land. If tunnels, cuttings and embankments were required, the surveyor would endeavour to make sure that soil excavated could be used in a nearby embankment. These plans, known as Deposited Plans, were placed with the local authority and Parliament. After the passing of the Act, with at least some of the capital raised, a contractor had to be found to

Boring Chedworth Tunnel on the Midland & South Western Junction Railway. Author's collection

carry out the work; those companies with less money would seek a contractor willing to work for shares rather than for cash.

Work usually began with the ceremonial turning of the first turf, a highly decorated spade being used to lift a sod into an equally ornate wheelbarrow.

Boring Hunting Butts Tunnel on the Cheltenham to Honeybourne line, 1906. Author's collection

Construction of the Cheltenham to Honeybourne line viewed from St George's Road Bridge, Cheltenham, February 1906. Author's collection

Navvy accommodation at Toddington, 1904. The goods shed is in the centre-left background. Author's collection

This was often done by the company's chairman or his wife. After the ceremony the directors and local dignitaries dined. The contractor set to work and was likely to meet difficulties – shortage of workers or materials, hard rock in an unexpected place that had to be cut through, or fluid clay that refused to stay in place. As a railway company might be unable to raise enough money to pay the contractor, or the contractor himself might go bankrupt, Parliament wisely decided that a railway company must deposit a sum of money, so that in the event of failure to complete the line after work had started, those funds deposited could be used to re-instate the property purchased compulsorily from the landowners. The Act of Parliament stipulated that a line should be completed within a certain period of time and quite often, because of various difficulties, the railway was forced to apply to Parliament for an extension of time and not infrequently for an increase in capital to cover unforeseen costs.

When the contractor completed the line and before it could be opened to passenger traffic, an inspection had to be undertaken for the Board of Trade through an officer of the Royal Engineers. He went over the line testing bridge and other structures, making sure that the signalling was adequate for safety and the stations had suitable facilities. Usually at least one fault was discovered. If it was minor the Board of Trade granted a certificate subject to its correction; but in the event of a major criticism, re-inspection was required before the line could be opened.

On the opening day the directors and local dignitaries travelled over the line, dining afterwards. If the railway was a local one, it was usually worked by a larger company to make the business more economic. That was because, although perhaps the line might require only one engine and two passenger coaches to work normal services, at least one more engine would be needed as a spare when the other engine was having a boiler wash-out or undergoing repair. On market days, fair days and Bank Holidays two coaches might prove insufficient. Some goods traffic required special rolling stock and it would be uneconomic to invest capital in something used only occasionally. To obviate such difficulties a small company therefore usually arranged for a larger company with larger resources to work the line for a percentage of the gross receipts. Some lines were far from profitable, ordinary shareholders rarely or never receiving a dividend, and it often happened that eventually a small railway was purchased by the working company, the payment usually less than its building cost.

In the early 1900s rail motors came into use, some of the first in

Admission ticket to dinner following the cutting of the first sod of the Stonehouse & Nailsworth Railway.

STONEHOUSE & NAILSWORTH RAILWAY.

(CUTTING THE FIRST SOD.)

DINNER TICKET.

SUBSCRIPTION ROOMS, NAILSWORTH,

MONDAY, FEBRUARY 22, 1864,

at **THREE o'Clock.**

Admit Wᵐ A. E. Smith

PROCESSION at One o'Clock,
(from the Subscription Rooms.)
CEREMONY at Two o'Clock.

the country being used in the Stroud Valley. A rail motor was a passenger coach and locomotive contained on the same underframe. It was designed so that when going boiler-first the engine would be at the front, but when returning the driver could walk to what had been the rear and drive from a special control compartment, the fireman remaining at the other end. The use

Steam railcar No 1 at Stonehouse circa 1903. The vertical boiler is in the compartment behind the fireman standing in the doorway. Michael Farr collection

of a rail motor obviated the time and trouble needed to run an engine round its train at the end of every journey. When a rail motor service was introduced, unmanned halts were opened at places where traffic was insufficient to warrant a staffed station.

Rail motors were found to lack flexibility. If, on (say) a market day, the number of passengers quadrupled, a rail motor could not cope as it was only powerful enough to draw one trailer. As a railway therefore required a locomotive and coaches standing by for such an eventuality, any saving made by the rail motor was lost.

20hp GWR Milnes-Daimler bus CO 84 stands at the Chalford terminus, 31 March 1905. Author's collection

The solution was a push-pull or auto train. An engine stayed at one end of the train and on the return journey, the driver could control his engine from a special compartment at what had been the rear by means of mechanical rods or compressed air.

The year 1923 brought Grouping when, apart from very minor lines, all railway companies became part of one of the Big Four: The Great Western Railway, the London, Midland & Scottish Railway (LMS); the London & North Eastern Railway (LNER) and the Southern Railway (SR). The GWR was the only railway to retain its old name, the other main company in Gloucestershire, the Midland Railway, becoming part of the LMS. With Nationalisation on 1 January 1948 the GWR became British Railways Western Region, and the LMS the London Midland Region, though minor area changes were made.

Railways were quick to spot the bus competitor and themselves participated in road transport. The first railway bus in Gloucestershire was that between Stroud and Painswick, inaugurated in lieu of constructing a light railway.

From 1928 legislation permitted railways to purchase large, but not controlling, shareholdings in existing bus companies. The GWR reached agreement with the National Omnibus & Transport Company and the Western National was set up to run bus services in GWR territory, the railway agreeing to transfer its road motor services to that company in return for a half share, the Western National undertaking to co-ordinate rail and road services and not to compete with the railway.

In addition to bus competition, the increase in private car ownership in the 1950s and 1960s was another reason for the decline in the number of rail passengers and many of the poorly-frequented stations closed. The smaller stations remaining open were generally unstaffed, passengers purchasing their tickets from the conductor-guard on the diesel multiple unit pay trains. Freight traffic also declined because of increased use of road vehicles, especially at times when railwaymen were on strike, their actions permanently damaging business. The swing to the use of electricity, North Sea gas and oil for heating brought a decrease in the once very heavy coal traffic to almost every station. Fifty years ago railways carried relatively small loads to a variety of destinations; today the railways are mainly bulk carriers of stone, steel, cars, coal and oil.

3 The Midland Railway Main Line: Bristol to Gloucester

THE COALPIT HEATH collieries were nine miles north of Bristol and the pit owners sought to increase profits by improving transport to Bristol, as cart or packhorse proved expensive. Onwards from 1803 many proposals were made, but proved abortive. The Bristol & Gloucestershire Railway suggested in 1827 was successful. An Act of 19 June 1828 authorised the

Cab view from an Up train approaching Staple Hill Tunnel 1963. W.F.Grainger

railway to be built from an Avon Street depot at Bristol Harbour. The northern half of the line was to be shared with the Avon & Gloucestershire Railway (AGR), a concern promoted by the Kennet & Avon Canal. This northern half was opened with the AGR in July 1832. The Bristol & Gloucestershire had used all its funds, so an Act of 26 March 1834 allowed the company to issue further shares. On 27 December 1834 it was announced that 282ft of the 515yd long Staple Hill Tunnel had been cut. Work completed, the line opened 6 August 1835.

Shareholders and friends were carried in adapted coal wagons, while ladies were favoured and carried in closed cars with green baize seats. Each wagon was drawn by a horse. The lineside was crowded with spectators anxious to see Bristol's first railway and the procession took three hours to cover the nine miles. The line's opening reduced, by five to six shilllings, the price of coal in Bristol which had been from sixteen to twenty shillings.

The *Bristol Gazette* reported:

'The most interesting part of the journey was the descent of the inclined plane [The 1 in 55 incline between Lawrence Hill Junction and Fishponds], where the horses were removed and carriages impelled forward by force of gravitation. For some distance they proceeded at the rate of a quick trot, but so great was the command by which the guides [brakesmen] were possessed, by means of a lever acting upon the wheels, that though even here several stoppages took place, there was not the least danger of a collision.'

The gauge was 4ft 8 in and the cast iron rails were fixed to stone blocks by chairs. The track was single line and rules stated that if two trains met between passing loops, the train proceeding to Coalpit Heath was required to return to the nearest loop. In 1835 a locomotive built by Bond & Windwood was tried, but exploded after being modified to increase its speed in order to make two, rather than one, trip daily.

On 1 July 1839 an Act was passed permitting the Bristol & Gloucester Railway (BGR) to absorb the Bristol & Gloucestershire and extend the line to Standish where it would join the Cheltenham & Great Western Union Railway (CGWUR) – see page 61 – and possess running powers to Gloucester. On 9 September 1839 I. K. Brunel was appointed engineer. In 1841 work was started building a standard gauge line, but then at a meeting on 29 March 1843 it was suggested that broad gauge would be an advantage so that passengers could travel in a through coach from Exeter to Gloucester. Brunel was in favour of the change, but the chairman, George Jones, against. Earthworks were sufficiently wide to allow broad gauge to be laid, as the only additional cost over a standard gauge line was an approximate cost of £5,000 for the extra ballast required. Offset against this was a saving of £30,000 by not needing to lay a third rail from Standish to Gloucester to accommodate the broad gauge CGWUR. The meeting decided to adopt broad gauge and extend the BGR to the GWR at Bristol, Temple Meads.

Ex-Bristol & Gloucester Railway broad gauge locomotive and coaches at Barnstaple in the 1850s. Author's collection

In November 1844 the Bristol Infirmary informed the BGR that 13 navvies had been 'expensive casualties', so the company added £20 to its normal subscription of £5 5s 0d.

The BGR opened on 6 July 1844, thus completing rail communication from Newcastle upon Tyne to Exeter. The opening of the BGR caused the withdrawal of three of the six stage coaches on the route.

Towards the end of 1844 talks were made for combining the BGR with the Birmingham & Gloucester Railway, but this union was swamped by something more dramatic. The GWR made an offer for the two companies and two of the Birmingham directors travelling to a meeting with the GWR directors at Paddington, were in the same compartment with John Ellis, deputy chairman of the MR. Naturally they discussed business and this resulted in the MR making a better offer than that of the GWR. This was accepted and the MR's lease of the Bristol & Birmingham Railway commenced on 1 July 1845. This move was ratified by Parliament 3 August 1846.

The BGR adopting broad gauge meant that there was necessarily a change of gauge at Gloucester for passengers and goods travelling between Bristol and Birmingham and vice versa. Going northwards, passengers simply stepped out of a BGR train and crossed the platform to Birmingham & Gloucester coaches, but those travelling southwards had to walk from one side of the station to the other. Matters were further confused by the fact that the station had three clocks set at three different times: Birmingham time for the Birmingham & Gloucester; Bristol time for the BGR and London time for the GWR, which by then had taken over the CGWUR. Transfer of goods took an average of 50 minutes for a 5 ton wagon.

As the MR was a standard gauge line, its acquisition of a broad gauge line necessitated an Act of 14 August 1848 to allow the MR to construct an independent line between Gloucester and Standish and lay mixed gauge onwards to Bristol. On 22 May 1854 this standard gauge line was opened and a journey between Birmingham and Bristol was speeded by the ten to fifteen minutes formerly occupied in changing trains at the break of gauge. The MR sold its redundant broad gauge stock to the contractor, Brassey, who used some of it on the North Devon Railway.

The GWR held running powers over the BGR, so the broad gauge had to remain. In later years the GWR found these powers most useful such as when the Severn Tunnel was closed for maintenance, trains could travel between South Wales and Bristol via the Severn Bridge, or Gloucester, while in 1908 the Bristol to Gloucester line was used by a Wolverhampton to Bristol express.

Following the withdrawal on 6 March 1966 of the Bristol to Bath passenger service via Mangotsfield and the general reduction in traffic over the line, Lawrence Hill Junction to Mangotsfield North Junction was closed 29 December 1969, trains running from Bristol to Yate via the GWR route via Filton. The line beyond Mangotsfield North was retained for use by trains carrying coal to Bath gas works, but when the Bath branch closed entirely on 31 May 1971, the track between Yate and Mangotsfield was retained for engineer's use, but subsequently closed south of the M4 motorway. In 1986 the formation became part of a walkway and cycle path.

Tickets from Gloucestershire stations.

Bristol to Gloucester passenger trains used Bristol, Temple Meads, but goods were dealt with across the Avon at St Philip's, while at the river itself was Avonside Wharf with facilities for loading/unloading barges, the MR keeping a fleet of these. Goods sensitive to the weather could be transferred at a covered dock. The single platform St Philip's station opened 2 May 1870 mainly for use by Bristol to Bath trains. Due to the enlargement of Temple Meads in 1935, it was declared redundant and closed 21 September 1953. Nearby was Barrow Road locomotive depot.

Fishponds station, with a ridge and furrow roof similar to St Philip's, opened 1 April 1886 to cater for the expansion of Bristol and a siding led to the Avonside Engine Company's locomotive works. Staple Hill station, opened 1 November 1886, set in a cutting, had its offices set above at street level. Because Staple Hill Tunnel was originally single track width, when widened its ventilating shafts became offset.

A new Mangotsfield station opened 4 August 1869, together with the branch to Bath. It had six platforms – two for each of the main lines and a bay platform for Mangotsfield to Clifton Down trains, plus an Up loop platform on the Gloucester line. The roof was longitudinal rather than the usual MR ridge and furrow. In addition to its use as a junction station for passengers changing trains, some employees at the adjacent Carson's chocolate factory travelled by rail. The original Mangotsfield station was at the North Junction where the Avon & Gloucestershire Railway originally diverged. The old station closed to passenger traffic when the new opened.

Jubilee class 4-6-0 No 5606 *Falkland Islands* south of Mangotsfield working the 2.52pm Bristol to Gloucester stopping train, 14 May 1936. It is fitted with an indicator shelter. Author's collection

Cab view from Class 5 2-6-0 No 2900 approaching Mangotsfield with an Up stopping train, March 1964. The Gloucester line curves left and the Bath branch, right. W.F.Grainger

The triangular junction at Mangotsfield was used for turning locomotives when a turntable was under repair, or a whole train in the case of the Travelling Post Office. Class 2P 4-4-0 No 40700, an S&D class 7F 2-8-0 and Class 4 2-6-0 No 43014 have arrived from Bath circa 1950 for this manoeuvre. Downend Local History Society

Westerleigh Sidings immediately south of the junction of the Coalpit Heath branch, opened in 1900 to ease goods traffic congestion at Bath and Bristol. With the rundown of freight traffic it closed 19 January 1965, though in 1985 part was used as a refuse terminal where rubbish containers were placed

BRITISH RAILWAYS BOARD (W) BR 4403/6

ISSUED AT..........MANGOTSFIELD..........

SINGLE TICKET   CI 02388

DATE 25th July 19 64 VALID FOR 3 Days

FROM Mangotsfield

TO Birmingham

VIA Bristow

For alternative routes, see Book of Routes

Description	Class	No. of Passengers (To be shown in words)	Fare	£	s.	d.
ORDINARY						
† FORCES DUTY :- OFFICERS			–	–	–	–
OTHER RANKS			–	–	–	–
FORCES LEAVE						
OTHERS (Insert details) P.W.	2nd one				5	3
†Warrant No............		............Amount Paid			5	3
		............Booking Clerk				

NOT TRANSFERABLE

This ticket is issued subject to the Bye-laws, Regulations and Conditions contained in the Publications and Notices of or applicable to the British Railways Board.

A handwritten Privilege Rate ticket for Mangotsfield to Birmingham, issued by Stationmaster Ron Price.

(Left) 8750 class 0-6-0PT No 3696 at Mangotsfield with snow plough, 4 March 1965. It had been used to deliver wages to signalmen from Yate to Charfield and was being turned on the triangle in order to proceed to Thornbury. Michael Culham/Colin Roberts collection

(Right) The old station at Mangotsfield North 21 April 1960. The left hand building contains the offices of the Mangotsfield Coal Company. The wagon is a WW2 Ministry of Transport vehicle. Author

on rail to be sent to landfill at Calvert, Buckinghamshire. On 1 March 1991 another part of the site was opened as an oil distribution terminal.

At Yate Junction, routes were designed so that a train from the MR or GWR could leave or join without crossing the path of another. Yate, like the

Westerleigh sidings 21 April 1960. The line to Coalpit Heath branched off at the far end of the yard and curved left. Author

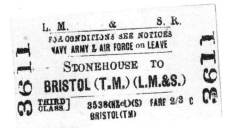

No 60033 *Anthony Ashley Cooper* arrives at the Murco Depot, Westerleigh, 1 March 1991, testing the new track with an empty tanker. Author

Class 8F 2-8-0 No 48336 passes below the Paddington to South Wales line at Westerleigh, 21 April 1960. Author

Class 4F 0-6-0 No 44209 working the 6.20am Gloucester Eastgate to Bristol Temple Meads, snowed up at Yate South Junction 31 December 1962. It was firmly fixed in the drift for six hours. A man is attempting to free a frozen signal. Colin Roberts collection

other BGR stations, was of typical Brunellian design. To make use of space, short sidings radiated from a wagon turntable. It closed to passengers 4 January 1965, as did the other stations between here and Gloucester, but as housing at Yate grew, a new station was opened 11 May 1989.

Wickwar Tunnel is 1,401yd in length and beyond was the low, brick-built station, squeezed between the platform and road. Charfield had a more substantial building. Berkeley Road had four platforms: two for the main line and two for the Sharpness branch. The opening of the Dursley & Midland Junction Railway 18 September 1856 coincided with the opening of Coaley station at the junction. Just to the north of this site, Cam & Dursley station opened 29 May 1994. The next station, Frocester, closed 11 December 1961.

Going on leave

Members of the Royal Flying Corps on the Up platform, Yate during WW1. Author's collection

ENQUIRY NOTE TO *CARDIFF GNL*   E.R.O. 21603   Reference

PARCELS DEPT

L M S—MISSING LUGGAGE, PARCELS, Etc.

YATE

From_____ Office_____ 13 NOV 1962 Station

BR. RLYS. (W)

Name of Owner or Contignee *MRS ROBERTS.*

Name of Sender _____

Missing Article *1 Pair Navy Blue, leather, lined*
(Give full description of exterior
and contents when possible) *winter gloves - average size.*

Addresses, Labels,
Marks and Initials _____

Lost on *9TH NOVEMBER 1962* Per* *2.35 P.M.*

From† *BRISTOL TM*   To *CARDIFF GNL or in*

If found, sent to *YATE.*   *Cardiff Gnl Waiting Room.*

* Give Train.   † Give starting and destination stations
State whether booked parcel, P.L.A., D.L., C.L., or Passenger's Accompanied Luggage and where loaded
Reply by writing across this form

Enquiry note for missing luggage Yate to Cardiff General.

Stonehouse was the junction with the Nailsworth & Stroud branches. The goods yard became Stonehouse Coal Concentration Depot 7 October 1966, but with the change of domestic heating from open fires to the central variety, demand decreased and the depot closed in 1989. At Standish the line from Swindon joined, four tracks running to Gloucester, though the line was reduced to double track in September 1968. In quadruple track days, unofficial racing took place between GWR and MR trains. Haresfield station was unusual in that it was only served by MR trains; also its Down platform

On 18 April 1952 Driver John Richmond rests on his 6 ton Scammell mechanical horse built in 1936. Notice the starting handle by his left hand. The single head lamp left much to be desired on unlit country roads. The cab bonnet is of rubber. Colin Roberts

A Torquay & Weston super Mare to Wolverhampton express hauled by 4-4-0 No 3812 *County of Cardigan* near Yate Junction 30 June 1925. H.G.W.Household

was devoid of a waiting shelter. At Quedgeley during WW1 about 5,000 workers were brought to a munitions factory daily by the MR, a special workers' platform opening 13 December 1915. During WW2 the site became an RAF store.

The BGR station at Gloucester had three tracks and being a terminus it meant that through trains such as Bristol to Birmingham, required reversal. On 12 April 1896 a through station was opened. Its architecture was in the domestic style and had typical MR ridge and furrow roof. The station was linked with the GWR station by a very long footbridge. This station, latterly known as Eastgate, was closed 1 December 1975 and all traffic concentrated on the former GWR station.

BR Standard class 5 4-6-0 No 73138 from Derby shed, working the 2.40pm Worcester to Temple Meads, passes below a combined aqueduct and footbridge at the south portal of Wickwar Tunnel, 12 August 1961. Author

Fireman's view of Wickwar Tunnel from an Up train, 1963. W.F.Grainger

Charfield station, view Up circa 1910. A horse box stands in the loading dock at the far end of the platform. Author's collection

Berkeley Road view Down 27 June 1964. BR Standard Class 5 4-6-0 No 73021 works an Up stopping train. The running-in board reads: 'Berkeley Road change for Sharpness' – 'Lydney' has been painted out due to the destruction of the Severn Bridge. W. Potter

Coaley Junction: view Up from a Down train 16 May 1959. 16XX class 0-6-0PT No 1605 stands on the Dursley branch. R.E.Toop

Frocester, view Down 27 June 1962. Notice the wagon turntable allowing access to the goods shed and short sidings. Lower left are trap points in case a vehicle started to run from the siding towards the main line. Author

Haresfield, view Up circa 1900. The platforms are of timber. Author's collection

Cab view of Barton Street Junction signal box from a Jubilee class engine, view Down, April 1964. Due to space constraints, the signal box is necessarily elevated. W.F.Grainger

1853 class 4-2-2 No 94 (right) at Gloucester circa 1905. Author's collection

4-2-2- No 676 at Gloucester with an up express circa 1909. Author's collection

4 The Midland Railway Main Line: Gloucester to Ashchurch

THE GLOUCESTER & Cheltenham Tramway was the first rail link between these towns, the Act being passed 28 April 1809. The first stone sleeper block was laid 21 November that year and the line opened 4 June 1811, though a branch from Cheltenham to Leckhampton Quarry had opened 2 July 1810. This horse-worked line was a great success, hauling about 25,000 tons of coal annually and paying shareholders a dividend of six per cent. On 28 January 1836 the Cheltenham & Great Western Union Railway purchased it for £35,000. The next day the CGWUR and the Birmingham & Gloucester Railway agreed to build a joint line between Cheltenham and Gloucester. This opened 4 November 1840, but did not use the tramway formation whose traffic continued. After 1854 the tramway's income only just exceeded expenditure and an Act for abandonment received Royal Assent 1 August 1859. The line was auctioned 19 April 1861 and most

Medallion struck to commemorate the *Royal William* locomotive on the Cheltenham & Gloucester Railway. Courtesy Engineering

28

of the tramway plates sold for further use on a tramway in the Forest of Dean. They were flanged and used by wagons with plain wheels. The gauge was 3ft 6 in.

Although tramway drivers were required by byelaw to walk beside their horses, the temptation to ride was irresistible. Riding was banned because the shafts were fixed to the front of the tram by a transom pin and the breakage of a pin would throw a driver sitting on the shafts right in front of the wagon and the consequences of this could be serious. This happened in September 1848, the *Cheltenham Examiner* reporting: 'Deceased was in the employ of Mr Jordan, coal merchant…He had been repeatedly warned by his master not to ride on the shafts on pain on dismissal from his service; but in spite of these warnings he persisted in this common but dangerous practice.'

It was not only drivers who receive injuries. In October 1827 'A little boy named Samuel Poulton was riding on a railway tram loaded with coal, one of the large pieces was shook off, which fell upon his thigh and fractured it.' On an earlier occasion 'Thomas Fletcher, a little boy about seven years of age, was left to take care of five trams on the railway road, when endeavouring to stop the horses, he by some means got underneath and they went over him.'

Two trams were the maximum load for one horse, a return trip of 17 miles from Cheltenham to Gloucester and back being a day's work. Loaded trams had precedence over empties, the latter being required to wait in a passing loop for an oncoming loaded train.

Benjamin Newmarch who had leased the tolls on the line, made an abortive trial of a novel steam locomotive. The patent of an American, Major M'Curdy, instead of a conventional boiler, which in those days of primitive technology was liable to explode, steam was generated on the flash principle whereby a small volume of water in a coil was turned instantly to steam, rather like some gas-fired water heaters today. This design failed through its inability to produce sufficient steam. During the winter of 1831-2, *Royal George* was tried, a conventional 0-6-0 designed by Henry Taylor and built by the Neath Abbey Ironworks in 1831. Although the locomotive was a success, the cast iron permanent way was of insufficient strength to support it and the experiment abandoned, horse traction continuing. C. E. Stretton, not an historian famed for accuracy, claimed that in 1839-40 J. E. McConnell, locomotive superintendent of the Birmingham & Gloucester, fitted flanged tyres on the wheels and eventually *Royal William* was broken up at Bromsgrove about 1842.

In 1836 a survey was made for a potential railway between Birmingham and Gloucester, the section in Gloucestershire entering just north of Ashchurch. Unlike some bills, it sped through Parliament and was passed on 22 April 1836. Delays were experienced through some landowners trying to be too greedy. One demanded £3,027, the Birmingham & Gloucester offered £650 and arbitrators awarded £752. All land purchased, the contractors began work in 1838. On 1 June 1840 a party of directors travelled by train from Cheltenham to Bromsgrove and the 31 miles between these stations were opened for passenger traffic 24 June 1840. Down trains used Birmingham time and up trains Cheltenham and Gloucester time. The line opened to Birmingham 17 August 1841. Due to lack of sidings, only a limited amount of freight could be carried.

The Birmingham & Gloucester terminus at Gloucester had two platform roads and two central carriage sidings, all covered by a train shed. The first station north of Gloucester was Churchdown. It had no goods facilities and closed to passengers 2 November 1964. Cheltenham Lansdown station is a fine building in classical style. Unusually it was adapted from an existing mansion set 1¼ miles from the town, so fitted the stipulation that the station should be at a 'respectable distance' from the town centre. Unfortunately an insensitive BR removed an exterior colonnade in the nineteen-fifties. The main platforms, originally covered with a train shed, were later shielded by ridge and furrow awnings. The station is particularly busy on race days and until the development of road transport, horses arrived by rail, nannies bringing children to see them being loaded and unloaded. Water columns at Cheltenham were marked with a broad red band as they were supplied with expensive mains water and therefore were only to be used in an emergency.

Cheltenham, High Street station opened 14 January 1890 and closed 1 July 1910. Cleeve station closed to passengers 20 February 1950. Ashchurch station was interesting as at the north end of the platforms, until 5 May 1957 the Tewkesbury to Evesham line crossed the Birmingham & Gloucester on the level. Ashchurch closed to passengers 15 November 1971. It re-opened 30

Queen Victoria changing gauge at Gloucester 29 September 1849. She has left her standard gauge train and is about to enter the broad gauge Royal Train. Author's collection

The exterior of the Birmingham & Gloucester station at Gloucester December 1896. Author's collection

Cheltenham station exterior circa 1850. Author's collection

The Royal Train passes Cheltenham 29 September 1849. Author's collection

View back over
the tender from
BR Standard Class
9 2-10-0 No
92151 hauling a
Down coal train
1964.
W.F.Grainger

Churchdown in
double track days.
Author's collection

Churchdown 16
April 1953 after
quadrupling.
Dr A.J.G.Dickens

May 1997, the station replacement costing £868,000 and expenditure on roads and car park approximately a further £350,000.

During World War Two a large US army camp was set up at Ashchurch. As the camp was muddy, soldiers wore galoshes over their shoes and left them in a hedge before boarding a train. On return, too drunk to retrieve them, some were left and railwaymen, to ease footwear rationing, went round finding a pair of the correct size. North of the station sidings served the MR provender store, a large building later taken over by the Dowty Group.

Left: Churchdown being quadrupled in 1942: two new side spans extend the existing bridge. Author's collection

Right: To widen the embankment for quadruple track, a borrow pit has been created on the right. Author's collection

Ashchurch: an outside frame 0-6-0 stands on the right; the Tewkesbury branch curves left. Note the three lamp pots in the coach roof. Author's collection

Ashchurch: the Tewkesbury to Evesham branch line crosses the main line, 16 April 1953. Dr A.J.G Dickens

5 Midland Railway Branches

The Bath Branch

IN 1812 THE Kennet & Avon Canal surveyed a line from Coalpit Heath to the Avon near Keynsham. Insufficient funds were subscribed, so the project foundered. When the Bristol & Gloucestershire scheme was proposed, the Kennet & Avon communicated with that company and proposed a branch line, the Avon & Gloucestershire Railway (AGR) from Mangotsfield to the river. The Act received Royal Assent 19 June 1828. 10 January 1831 2½ miles of the railway were opened and served intermediate collieries. The northern portion of the Bristol & Gloucestershire was opened by 17 July 1832 enabling the whole of the AGR to be opened. This led to a reduction in the price of coal along the Kennet & Avon by 3 to 4 shillings per ton. As Avon Wharf was better suited to vessels going upstream to Bath, a short spur was built to Londonderry Wharf, more convenient for Bristol traffic. Work on building this new line began in December 1832 and was completed by July 1833, though the opening of the Bristol & Gloucestershire to Bristol in August 1835 drastically reduced the weight of coal passing down the AGR, 1,000 tons per week fell to 200 tons weekly in 1843.

When the BGR made the Mangotsfield to Westerleigh section broad gauge, this length became the first mixed gauge section in the country. The tramway's rails were laid between the broad gauge rails. Horses were able to travel over the 2 ⅝ miles of common route in under an hour and as the BGR trains ran at intervals of not less than 2 hours 20 minutes, there was no problem with horse and steam traction over the same length.

On 1 July 1851 the Kennet & Avon Canal was taken over by the GWR. As most of the pits were worked out, an Act of 5 July 1865 allowed the AGR to be closed, but the track remained in situ. California Colliery at Oldland re-opened in 1881 and the line southwards was repaired. The last coal on the tramway travelled on 30 January 1904 and most of the rail was lifted for salvage during WW1.

At Willsbridge the portal of the 156yd long tunnel remains, with an impressive rock cutting at its far end. The line then ran along the shelf of a steep hillside on a notable retaining wall. It passed through a 30ft tunnel and a further tunnel 73yd in length which the MR strengthened when it built its line above. The AGR joined the Bristol & Gloucestershire at Mangotsfield North Junction

With the opening of the BGR, it was found desirable to create a link line to Bath to offer a more direct line so that passengers from that city travelling northwards could avoid travelling via Bristol. This Act received Royal Assent 21 July 1864. Construction work started November 1865 and as the GWR had already seized the best route along the Avon valley, the MR was forced to build six two-span bridges across the river in five miles. The line opened on 4 August 1869 and traffic developed as expected when the Somerset & Dorset Railway opened to Bath on 20 July 1874, thus placing the Mangotsfield to Bitton line on a through route between the Midlands and the South coast.

By the 1930s the line's railway bridges were insufficiently strong to support the larger engines coming into production, so a bridge replacement programme took place. Fortunately this work was completed just prior to WW2 when the line became of strategic importance, particularly in the weeks before and after the D-Day landings.

Unfortunately in the 1960s, traffic declined when passengers were booked by alternative routes, often longer and costing the passenger a higher fare. The line became uneconomic, so passenger services were withdrawn on 7 March 1966. Goods traffic continued, but on 5 May 1968 the branch was singled. 3,200 tons of coal still arrived weekly for Bath gas works until the

Warmley, view south from the cab of a tank engine. Notice the small, timber-built goods shed and loading dock, right. W.F.Grainger

introduction of North Sea gas caused the closure of the works in May 1971, so the branch closed 28 May 1971. Some of the track lifted the following year was used to relay the line to Tytherington (see page 39).

The Bristol Suburban Railway Society, now the Avon Valley Railway, reopened Bitton station in 1972 and gradually extended track to Oldland Common and then southwards to the first river bridge. In 1979 the formation between Bath and Mangotsfield was turned into a footpath and cycle track which sees considerable use.

The first station on the branch was Warmley which had timber buildings, the waiting room on the former Down platform is still extant and used as a café for footpath users. To the south, the signal box remains as a listed building. Apart from dealing with general merchandise, the yard despatched bricks and pipes; red, blue, green and yellow ochre and Douglas motorcycles. Oldland Common, with sleeper-built platforms, opened 2 December 1935 and was the only station on the line electrically lit. Perhaps curiously, it was used by more passengers than its parent station, Bitton. The line passed through the pennant rock Bitton Cutting from which stone was taken for constructing most of the stations and bridges on the branch. Bitton station has a typical MR twin pavilion style main building. One rather unusual traffic sent from the station was moulding sand to Sheffield. Immediately south of the station was an impressive embankment about 1½ miles in length. At its end is the 3-arch River Boyd Viaduct, followed almost immediately by a steel bridge of two 87ft spans which takes the line into Somerset.

The timber platforms at Oldland Common, view Down circa 1963. Lens of Sutton

890 class 2-4-0 No 89 arrives at Bitton with a Down train circa 1908. Author's collection

A farm train at Bitton, September 1933. One wagon is carrying implements and in front of the cattle wagons on the left is a container laden with farm house furniture. The end of the passenger station building carries an advertisement for Lux soap flakes. Author's collection

The Thornbury Branch

Following the opening of the BGR in 1844, plans were made for a branch from Yate to Thornbury which, in addition to ordinary traffic, would have served an iron ore mine at Iron Acton and stone quarries at Tytherington. The Yate & Thornbury Act received Royal Assent 14 July 1864, the same day as the Mangotsfield to Bath Act. A further Act of 5 July 1865 authorised a branch to the iron ore mine at Frampton Cotterell.

Some landowners proved obstructive and not all the land could be purchased until 31 May 1867. Construction started 30 June 1867, and the branch opened 2 September 1872. The *Times & Mirror* had reservations about the usefulness of the line. After observing

Iron Acton, view Down 1932. The child's car is in a perilous position. Author's collection

Peak class diesel-electric No D192 crosses Iron Acton by-pass en route for Yate, 14 September 1973. W.H.Harbor

that hitherto passengers to Thornbury had to travel on the Bristol & South Wales Union Railway from Bristol to Patchway and then catch a bus, it continued: '...unless time is an object, it is very probable that this will continue to be a favourite route, for it is not only a pleasanter, but cheaper journey'. The MR return rail fare Bristol to Thornbury was 1s 5½ d compared with the return fare of 6d from Bristol to Patchway and 8d outside, or 10d inside return fare on the horse bus from Patchway to Thornbury.

Motor bus competition began on 5 February 1906 when the Bristol Tramways & Carriage Company operated a service linking Thornbury with the tram terminus at Horfield. Passenger trains were withdrawn 19 June 1944. From this date, parcels traffic to and from Tytherington and Thornbury was conveyed by freight train and except for coal traffic, Iron Acton station closed completely. (The Frampton Cotterell branch had closed 15 April 1878).

Tytherington, view Down circa 1960. Lens of Sutton

Special wartime traffic included military ambulance trains drawn by London & North Eastern Railway B12/3 class 4-6-0s carrying patients to Thornbury where they were taken by road to the US Army Hospital at Leyhill, adjoining Tortworth Court. From 1962, in addition to stone traffic from Tytherington, the branch was used to convey material for the construction of the Severn Bridge and the nuclear power station at Oldbury on Severn.

Thornbury closed to freight 20 June 1966, but stone trains continued to Grovesend Quarry until 24 November 1967. Track lifting started in September 1968. Then in 1970, Tytherington Quarry looked for markets further afield to be exploited when the M5 motorway contract finished. For such expansion, a rail link was required. Track relaying began in mid-April 1972 and the first train, its destination Milton Keynes, ran on 3 July 1972 almost a century after the original opening.

Class 4F 0-6-0 No 44466 enters Tytherington Tunnel with a Down train April 1964.
W.F.Grainger

DMU set B577 at Tytherington Quarry 9 June 1974 about to take quarry employees on a mystery tour. (It was to the Isle of Wight). Author's collection

The Engineer's Department wagons at Tytherington stone quarry circa 1910 have their axle boxes covered to prevent the entry of foreign bodies. Author's collection

The author on the footplate of Class 4F 0-6-0 No 44355 at Thornbury 17 August 1956. Author

Berkeley Road to Lydney

The Severn Bridge Railway was constructed to link the Severn & Wye Railway and the GWR at Lydney, with the MR at Berkeley Road, this offering the opportunity for ships to coal at Sharpness and the MR to gain access to the Forest of Dean coalfield. The Act authorising the railway received Royal Assent 18 July 1872.

The estimated cost of the line was £277,973 towards which the MR subscribed £50,000, the Gloucester & Berkeley Canal £50,000 and the Severn & Wye Railway £25,000. The GWR did not take up the offer of subscribing. It was debated whether a footbridge should be added to the structure at an additional cost of £10,000, but Gloucestershire County Council refused to put forward the money reasoning that if people desired to reach the other side they would go by train and not wish to walk.

The bridge building contract was let in March 1875 for £190,000 to the Hamilton Windsor Iron Works, Liverpool. They started work as soon as the contract was signed and on 3 June 1875 the first stone of the bridge was laid. The railway contract, also placed that March, was on Vickers & Cook,

0-6-0T *Friar Tuck*, later MR No 1124A, at Berkeley Road. It was built by the Avonside Engine Co, Bristol in 1870 for the broad gauge and converted to standard gauge two years later. Dr Budden

Parcels Way Bill.		GREAT WESTERN AND MIDLAND COMPANIES' SEVERN & WYE JOINT RAILWAY.				This Way Bill to be used for Traffic in quantities of less than 2 cwt.				
From		to		, on		Railway,				
	Train	day of		193	Via			(S.W. 9)		
No.	Description	Name	Address	Weight lbs.	Paid on £ s. d.	Paid £ s. d.	TO PAY £ s. d.	Excess Luggage £ s. d.	Remarks	
1										
2										
3										
4										
5										
			TOTAL ...							

Severn & Wye Joint Railway parcels waybill.

Severn & Wye Joint Railway passenger's acknowledgement for receipt of luggage.

(S.W. 322.)

SEVERN & WYE JOINT RAILWAY.

———————————————————Station,

————————————————————19

I declare, that through my own neglect, I have lost the Railway Company's Cloak Room Ticket No.——————————— issued to me————————————————on my depositing my Luggage, which Luggage consisted of——————————— ————————————and which I have since received.

————————————————————

Witness———————————————————

500—K 2-9-13—15070 &

14XX class 0-4-2T No 1401 at Berkeley Road with the 11.52am auto train to Lydney Town, 14 June 1958. No 1401 appeared in the film 'The Titfield Thunderbolt'. R.E.Toop

The atomic flask siding, Berkeley, 10 April 1991. Author

Sharpness station circa 1910 with an unusual brick waiting shelter in front of the signal box. The Severn Bridge is in the distance. Author's collection

Sharpness in single track days: 14XX class 0-4-2T No 1454 on 29 October 1960. Michael Jenkins

The sailing ship *Wolfe* built 1881, at Sharpness Docks apparently awaiting a consignment from the coke wagons. The wooden coal tip was rebuilt in concrete in 1900. P. White collection

Sharpness Docks 0-4-0ST shunter No 3, 20 May 1964,built by Avonside, Bristol in 1902. As it was scrapped on site circa May 1964, the photographer only just arrived in time. Rev Alan Newman

Sharpness scrapyard 20 May 1964: right to left, 4-6-0 No 4996 *Eden Hall*, No 5943 *Elmdon Hall* and No 4924 *Eydon Hall*. Rev Alan Newman

London, for £90,000, though the work was actually finished by Griffith Griffiths.

Bridge work started on the Sharpness shore where the currents were feeble. Cylinders were sunk and compressed air forced into them, thrusting out the water to enable sinkers to work on the bottom, sometimes 70ft below the surface of the water. Stages were constructed, a platform made and the spans erected on it. In the centre of the river, the scaffolding was insufficiently strong and was washed away by a spring tide. The tide normally rose 30ft in 2½ hours and this added to the difficulties. The contractors were up-to-date and used electric light for working at night.

The bridge was a series of iron bow-string girders resting on cast iron piers filled with concrete and rock. A felt lining inserted between the cast iron and the concrete, was intended to stop the cast iron cracking, but this idea was not a success and by 1960 most of the cylinders had been fractured by frost. The total length of the bridge, including the viaduct and swing span at the Sharpness end, was 4,162ft. When first painted, the lower part of the cylinders was black, the upper part chocolate and the girders cream, but latterly it was grey all over.

The swing span crossed the Gloucester & Berkeley Canal. It turned on a central masonry pier built between the canal and the Severn. It was moved

A train at Severn Bridge station circa 1905, heading to Sharpness. Author's collection

The Severn Bridge
with the Gloucester
& Berkeley Canal
in the foreground;
the swing span and
control cabin.
Author's collection

by a steam engine fixed in a glass-sided cabin on top of the girders above the railway and situated over the central pier. This building also contained signalling apparatus. The locking and turning mechanism was designed so that both could not be in gear at the same time and the bridge was locked by iron wedges lifting it on the masonry piers.

During the period when the engine driver, or signalman was on duty, the bridge was required to be kept closed across the canal, but when no one was in attendance, the span was kept open so that vessels could pass. A signal arm fixed to the bridge indicated to shipping whether it could be opened or not. Vessels requiring the span to be opened gave three whistles when they were at least 400yd away and, when the span was fully swung, the bridge operator replied with three whistles. Vessels too tall to pass under the bridge and seeing the signal against them, were required to stop at least 300yd from the bridge at a point indicated by a white post on the tow path.

An engine driver was required to be on duty on one of the day shifts in order to keep the engines and machinery in good repair; the signalman on the other shift assisted the driver in cleaning and coaling.

When closed for part of the night, the man on early turn had to have the engine in steam ready for swinging the span at least 20 minutes before the first train was due and the man on late turn was required to bank the fire after the last train had passed and the bridge swung open. One of the two boilers was used for a fortnight and then washed out, the other then being used.

The promoters spent £10,000 making the swing span wide enough for double track in case of future need, but time proved that their money was wasted.

On October 3 and 4 1879, Colonel Rich inspected the completed bridge on behalf of the Board of Trade to ensure it was safe for public traffic. Eight

MR goods engines weighing a total of between 300 and 400 tons stood on each girder in turn and were then run over the bridge at varying speeds. The deflection of one inch under this load was much less than expected.

Safety ensured, the bridge was opened on 17 October 1879, curiously enough exactly a century after the very first iron bridge in the world was constructed (at Ironbridge), which to add to the coincidence, was also across the Severn.

On the day the bridge opened, the Severn & Wye and the Severn Bridge companies amalgamated. The combined company failed to prosper and was placed in Chancery in 1883. Eventually the whole line was sold to the GWR and MR for £477,300, and, together with the already existing MR branch from Berkeley Road to Sharpness, became a joint line on 1 July 1894.

On Sundays when the Severn Tunnel was closed for inspection and repair, some trains from South Wales to England were diverted via the bridge, rather than through Gloucester. Between WW1 and WW2 the GWR wished to use heavier locomotives on these diverted trains, but the LMS, as successors to the MR, would not allow this. When it fell into the hands of British Railways, Western Region, this Derby regulation was abolished and heavier engines permitted. Moguls were the heaviest allowed and in 1960 Fairfields of Chepstow were at work strengthening the bridge in order for it to carry Castle class locomotives.

The death blow of the bridge came on the night of 25 October 1960 when a pier was struck and two spans destroyed by an oil tanker. Faced with a bill of £294,000 for replacing the broken spans, it was decided that the cost of repair could not economically be justified. Unfortunately for BR, under the Merchant Shipping Act, the limited liability for damage through collision did not exceed the sum equal to about 24 times the net registered tonnage of the

16XX class 0-6-0PT No 1627 about to collect the single line tablet from the Severn Bridge signalman, 19 July 1958. The Midland Railway signal box replaced the one in the previous view on 12 November 1911. R.E.Toop

vessel, or vessels. BR only received £5,000 compensation, while Fairfields, which lost plant to the value of £10,000, received just a little over £100.

BR took more than six years to make up its mind what to do with the bridge, and then in 1967 arranged with the Nordman Construction Company of Gloucester to dismantle and remove the bridge and masonry approach arches, the spans being recycled to form a road bridge in Chile.

The bridge had been struck by shipping no less than seven times between 1939 and 1961. At half tide the water rushed past the piers in a 10 knot millrace and if a boat struck the bridge at this speed just as a passenger train was crossing, the results would have been unthinkable.

The broken spans caused problems for scholars from Sharpness travelling to Lydney Grammar School. It meant that they had to travel via Gloucester, a round trip of 78 miles daily instead of the previous four miles each way across the bridge. The cost of a season ticket still worked out at less than two shillings a day.

14XX class 0-4-2T No 1401 working the 11.52am Berkeley Road to Lydney Town takes on water at Lydney Junction, 14 June 1958. R.E.Toop

During WW2 it was not unknown for pilots on training flights to dive Spitfires and Hurricanes between the bridge deck and the water. An onlooker admired them, until he saw men painting the bridge, hanging in their cradle while an aircraft flew within a few feet of them.

The Dursley Branch

Due to Dursley's location almost surrounded by hills, the town could not be served by the BGR's main line. Manufacturers in the area cast envious glances at their rivals in the Stroud Valley served by both rail and canal. Meetings were held and in due course the Dursley & Midland Junction Railway Act was passed on 9 May 1855. The impecunious company purchased second hand permanent way from the MR. The line opened to goods 25 August 1856 and to passengers 17 September 1856.

Twelve months' operation saw the company £1,000 in debt and, seeking economies, decided to work the line itself rather than having the MR carry out this task. It purchased a small 0-4-0ST for £434 10s 0d to draw two 4-wheeled coaches hired from the MR. Far from the financial situation improving, it grew worse, so the line was sold to the MR in 1860, shareholders losing £11 10s 0d on each £20 share. The passenger service was withdrawn 10 September 1962, but freight trains continued until 1 November 1966 and with the closure of Messrs Lister's siding, services finally ended 13 July 1970. The level crossing gates from Coaley Road and Cam are preserved by the Dean Forest Railway Society.

The Dursley branch train circa 1857. The 0-4-0ST built in 1856, probably by Stothert, Slaughter & Co, Bristol, was first used by the contractor. It eventually became MR No 156 and in December 1883,was sold to the Bridgewater Navigation Co Ltd, Runcorn, for £400. Author's collection

0-4-2T No 202 at Dursley circa 1866. Built in October 1851 as a 2-2-2WT by William Fairburn & Son for the Little North Western Railway, it became MR No 159 in June 1852, was rebuilt as a 0-4-2WT in June 1865, re-numbered 202 in May 1866 and broken up in October 1892. The first coach is a six-wheeler and the second a four-wheeler. Author's collection

The junction station at Coaley was unusual in that its buildings were set at right angles to the main line. The locomotive shed at Dursley pre-dated the railway, being economically converted from an existing structure.

In the latter days of the passenger service, one coach generally sufficed, and until 1957 was hauled by a class 1F 0-6-0T with no back to the cab, so that when running in reverse, which it did for half its life, the head and shoulders of the driver and firemen were exposed to the elements. These

Class 3F 0-6-0 No 43645 at Coaley Junction circa 1955. Author's collection

Class 1F 0-6-0T No 41720 crosses the partly-timber Quag Bridge with a mixed train, 10 October 1955. W. Potter

Class 1F 0-6-0T No 41720 at Cam with a train to Dursley. A van is carried as tail traffic behind the single passenger coach. Author's collection

Class 2F 0-6-0 No 58206 runs round its train at Dursley, 7 May 1955. R.E.Toop.

Class 1F 0-6-0T No 1720 (22B Gloucester) at Dursley circa 1947. Due to lack of space, no run-round loop could be provided here, necessitating the train backing out to the yard in order for the engine to run round. Author's collection

Class 2F 0-6-0 No 58206 at Dursley with the 8.15pm to Coaley Junction, 7 May 1955. Notice the briquettes in the tender. R.E.Toop

engines were known as 'Get wets'. In 1957 the branch was taken over by the Western Region which used a modern design of locomotive dating from only eight years before, but during the last few months, passenger trains were headed by a relatively large tender engine. The longest, or one of the longest trains, was on 2 June 1956 when a 15-coach Sunday School Outing special to Weston super Mare was worked on the branch by a Class 5 4-6-0 at one end and a Class 1F 0-6-0T at the other.

Stonehouse to Stroud and Nailsworth

An advertisement in the Stroud Journal 8 June 1867.

In the nineteenth century the valleys around Stroud and Nailsworth were hives of industry. The Cheltenham & Great Western Union Railway served the Stroud Valley and this made Nailsworth feel neglected. A scheme for building a line to Nailsworth was partly scuppered in 1854 due to religious prejudice, some members of the Parliamentary Committee rejecting the bill as the line would have offered greater facilities for attending a Roman Catholic church at Woodchester.

The Act eventually received Royal Assent 13 July 1863 to build a line from a junction with the MR at Stonehouse and it was the intention of the proprietors that it would be continued to Tetbury and Malmesbury before joining the GWR at Chippenham. The line's construction caused one householder problems. Excavations on the clay slope caused the foundations of his home to slip and forced him to take to bed the necessary tools required to open his bedroom door the next morning. The line opened to goods 1 February 1867 and passengers 4 February 1867. The company failed to succeed financially and was taken over by the MR in 1878.

The branch to Stroud was built to satisfy Stroud mill owners frustrated by the change of gauge at Gloucester and who demanded through trains. After several false starts, the

Act was passed 6 August 1880 for building a line from Dudbridge to Stroud. It proved highly expensive to construct, £37,198 for 1¼ miles, whereas many lines cost less than a third of this. It opened to goods 16 November 1885 and passengers 1 July 1886.

Both branches suffered from early bus competition which began in April 1908 and undercut railway fares. Passenger traffic was temporarily withdrawn on 16 June 1947 complying with Government instructions to reduce passenger mileage in order to counteract a post war fuel shortage. On 8 June 1949 it was announced that the passenger closure would be permanent. Goods traffic continued to flourish, though timber from Sharpness Docks to Stroud was lost to road about 1962 when the railway raised its tariff. The Nailsworth line had no less than five private sidings serving factories. The last freight train ran on both branches 1 June 1966.

Stations at Ryeford and Dudbridge were well-designed buildings in Cotswold stone, Nailsworth being particularly impressive as it was the headquarters of the Stroud & Nailsworth Railway. Nailsworth station still stands at the end of a long carriage drive. In front of the door is an arcade supported on leafy capitals, very similar to carvings in Stroud Parish church completed the year prior to the line's opening.

Left: A third class season ticket for Master C. P. Newman to travel between Woodchester and Ryeford, the station for Wycliffe College.

Right: His Majesty's Forces Overseas third class ticket from France to King's Stanley [Ryeford].

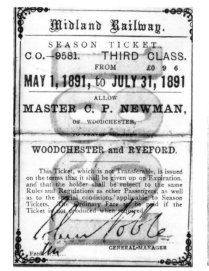

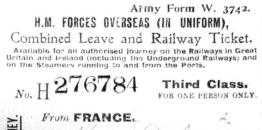

Class 1P 0-4-4T No 1330 enters Ryeford from Stroud, 28 May 1947. Notice the generously wide platform. R.J.Buckley

Dudbridge, view towards Stonehouse, 15 October 1955. W. Potter

A Bertram Mills' elephant arrives at Dudbridge, 1951. K. Ofield

Letter from the District Operating Superintendent's Office, Gloucester, to K. Ofield, Dudbridge station master.

E.R.O. 24169

LONDON MIDLAND AND SCOTTISH RAILWAY COMPANY

F. SPARKES,
District Operating Supt.,

Telephone: Gloucester 5171. Ext.............
Telegrams. "Operating, L M S Gloucester."

YOUR REFERENCE

OUR REFERENCE

G.Pad. 39.

DISTRICT OPERATING MANAGER'S OFFICE,
GLOUCESTER,

14th September, 19 5

Mr. Ofield,
Station Master,
DUDBRIDGE.

PERSONAL.

Dear Ofield,

Bertram Mills Circus Tour - 1951.

After having seen you a few days ago, I was in no doubt at all that you would see to it that the movement of the three Circus trains from your station would be carried out efficiently.

My confidence in you has been well confirmed and I should like to take this opportunity of specially thanking you and your staff for what I know to be a most creditable performance.

Your interest and cooperation with my District Inspector Hoss produced results which gave every satisfaction to the Circus Officials.

Please convey to all concerned my appreciation of such a splendid effort.

Yours sincerely,

Letter from the Chief Operating Manager's Office, Derby, 1 March 1934, offering G. Harrison a position as Porter at Dudbridge station at 40 shillings a week.

ERO.19826.

LONDON MIDLAND AND SCOTTISH RAILWAY COMPANY.

FROM CHIEF OPERATING MANAGER'S OFFICE

Office.

S.O.

19

Dear Sir,

      With further reference to your application for mployment;   I can now offer you a situation as _____ t _____ Station.

      The rate of pay will be _____ per _____.

      Should you decide to accept the situation on these terms, lease inform me upon what date you can enter upon your duties, nd I will then furnish you with instructions.

           Yours faithfully,

r. _____

Class 4F 0-6-0 No 44045 at Dudbridge Junction heads a train to Nailsworth 5 October 1962. The Stroud branch curves left. A coke wagon is behind the engine. W. Potter

0-6-0WT No 2008 outside Nailsworth engine shed, 1873. The passenger loop can be seen in the background at a higher level. Rev.W.V.Awdry collection

The station building at Woodchester opened 1 July 1867 some six months later than the others. It was of timber and unusual in being creosoted, rather than painted. At one period Woodchester enjoyed a considerable number of tourists visiting Amberley, the 'Enderley' of the novel *John Halifax, Gentleman*. Although passenger traffic slackened off latterly, the station was one of the busiest on the MR in Gloucestershire and for three consecutive years won a shield given to the station in the Gloucester District which handled the greatest volume of parcels traffic.

Class 1P 0-4-4T No 1364 at Nailsworth circa 1910 with a rake of six coaches comprising eight and six wheelers. The engine bears the '7' shed plate – Gloucester. On the far right, a point indicator can be seen placed at the end of the run-round loop. Author's collection

The staff at Woodchester circa 1910. MR posters advertise weekend tickets, a pantomime at Bristol, details of the train service in foggy weather and travel to Belfast and the North of England. Author's collection

The branch passenger platform at Stonehouse was separate from the main line platforms, but linked by a corrugated iron covered way. About half a mile east of Stonehouse was a siding to Stonehouse Wharf on the Stroudwater Canal. Beyond, the branch crossed the canal by a very oblique bridge.

Class 1P 0-4-4T No 1330 (22B Gloucester) at the branch platform, Stonehouse, with a train for Stroud, 28 May 1947. Notice the point indicator to the left of the buffers. On the right hand side of the smoke box is the push-pull apparatus. R.J.Buckley

The branch dealt with a great variety of traffic: timber, cornflour, stone, cattle food, printed paper, engineering products, cloth, rags, dyes, sausage skins and violin strings, wooden pattens, leather, incubators, pigs and bacon. Coal for the Stroud Gas Light & Coke Company travelled by canal until 1924 when a siding was laid to serve it. A wagon was run to the end of a chute where an hydraulic ram raised one end so that coal would fall out of the other. At the lower end of the chute, coal was released into 2ft gauge wagons which were hauled by an internal combustion engine across the River Frome to the gas works. An electrically powered capstan moved the standard gauge wagons along the siding. When the gas works closed 31 May 1956, the traffic of 7-8 wagons of coal daily, ceased.

The coal tippler, Stroud gas works. Coal from a standard gauge wagon is being tipped by a hydraulic ram into 2ft gauge hopper wagons, spring 1926. Author's collection

Approaching Stroud station was the 145yd long Wallbridge Viaduct. Some of its arches were bricked up and let to commercial firms – a few arches used as a cloth mill. The passenger station building was constructed of timber; after closure to passenger traffic, it was occupied by British Road Services. Another timber structure was the two-storey stable building, the dray horses climbing a zigzag path to their stables over the fodder stores and cart shed.

Class 1P 0-4-4T No 1361 at Stroud, heads a train to Dudbridge in the early nineteen-thirties. D. Thompson

The MR stables, Stroud. Vehicles are kept on the ground floor and horses in the first storey. Lionel Padin collection

The High Orchard Branch, Gloucester

The Gloucester & Berkeley Canal brought sea-going ships to Gloucester. In the late 1840s the Birmingham & Gloucester Railway opened a 250yd long link from its Gloucester station to the Gloucester & Cheltenham Tramway in order to carry goods to and from the docks direct in standard gauge wagons.

Class 0F 0-4-0T No 4153 (85B Gloucester) shunting on the Gloucester Docks branch near Southgate Street level crossing, 2 November 1962. Rev. Alan Newman

Hempstead Wharf sidings circa 1914. The siding on the left led to the gas works. Standing on the right is a ground frame hut. The Engineer's Department wagons, left, have their axle boxes covered to prevent foreign bodies entering. The rail-built stop block, left, is sturdily constructed. Author's collection

A locomotive not fitted with an ash box drew wagons on part of this journey, so dropped live embers on the track used for some years as a footpath. Ann Williams, aged six, played with these embers and ignited her frock causing fatal injuries.

A new branch from the main line at Tuffley Junction was opened to goods traffic on 24 May 1900. In 1913 a sub-branch served the gas works. A further line crossed Marsh Meadow to link with the GWR docks line. Many firms were served by the High Orchard branch, one being the Gloucester Railway Carriage & Wagon Works. The branch closed 1 October 1971.

The Tewkesbury Branch

Official details are vague, but the Ashchurch to Tewkesbury line was probably completed some time in 1839 and used to carry construction material for the Birmingham & Gloucester Railway. It was certainly open by 1 May 1840

The single coach 1.30pm Saturdays-only Upton on Severn to Ashchurch hauled by Class 3F 0-6-0T No 47422, at Tewkesbury 9 September 1960. The majority of locomotives in this class had only two coal rails, but a few, including No 47422 were fitted with six to enable a good supply of fuel to be carried. R.E.Toop

The 2.25pm Ashchurch to Tewkesbury on arrival 9 September 1960. R.E.Toop

The old station at Tewkesbury, closed 16 May 1864, seen here on 16 April 1955. Author's collection

when a permanent way train was involved in an accident killing two workmen. When the Cheltenham to Bromsgrove portion of the Birmingham & Gloucester was opened on 24 June 1840, a locomotive hauled a train of spectators from Tewkesbury to Ashchurch to see the first train, but the branch was not opened to regular traffic until 21 July 1840.

Trotman, the local carrier, for £250-300 per annum, provided horse power to haul the single carriage along the branch. First and second class passengers rode inside and third class outside. After 18 February 1844 horse traction ceased, apart from the connection with the Night Mail, the locomotive being serviced at this hour.

The opening of the Birmingham & Gloucester affected Tewkesbury innkeepers as most of the 30 daily stage coaches were withdrawn. A siding was laid to the quay to facilitate water/rail interchange. The original Tewkesbury station in High Street closed 16 May 1864 when the MR extended the line to the GWR at Great Malvern, a new Tewkesbury station being opened. Passenger services to Tewkesbury were withdrawn 14 August 1961, the Quay branch having been closed 1 February 1957 and the Tewkesbury branch closed to freight 2 November 1962.

6 GWR Main Lines: Kemble to Gloucester

IN JANUARY 1833 the first serious proposals for a line to link Bristol with London were put forward. That autumn some Cheltonians realised the benefit of a link line via Gloucester and Stroud. In 1835 Brunel was appointed the company's engineer, a sensible choice as he was also responsible for the Bristol to London line. A prospectus was published and although Cheltenham subscribed £212,800, Stroud £124,900 and Cirencester £85,000, Gloucester only subscribed £18,000.

There was certainly a demand for a railway as 23 horse-drawn wagons ran between Stroud and Cirencester to London weekly charging £5 per ton to London and £10 from London, whereas the railway promised a rate of only £1 16s 0d. Road transport was bad for cloth as bumpy roads wore holes in the bales, while in summer butter deteriorated in the heat and had to be sold as grease. Corn sent by water was often pilfered, whereas this was unlikely on a quick railway journey. Stage coaches took a day to reach the capital, whereas a railway would allow passengers to go up and back the same day.

Although most were in favour of the railway, the line was against the interests of a few, one being the Thames & Severn Canal which would lose much of its traffic. The other main opponent was Squire Gordon of Kemble who hated a railway spoiling his property. Both these antagonists were pacified by a gift of £7,500 each. The Cheltenham & Great Western Union Railway (CGWUR) Act passed on 21 June 1836, authorised the construction of a line from Cheltenham to Swindon and a branch from Kemble to Cirencester. The Act contained a clause stating that the railway would be run in a tunnel near Gordon's house so that it would be out of sight. When the line was opened he claimed that it was not out of sound, so the GWR arranged for a locomotive to let off steam. The company's solicitors waiting at Kemble House reported that although the wind was blowing from the direction of the station, the sound could only just be heard from outside the house, and not at all from its interior.

The line was too long too build as an entity and it was decided to complete the Swindon to Cirencester first and then use a road link to Stroud, Gloucester and Cheltenham. The resident engineer of this section was Charles Richardson who later became chief engineer to the Severn Tunnel and also designed the first cricket bat with a spliced cane handle.

Contractors began work in 1838, but wet weather in the first four months of 1840 caused earth slips. Eventually the line was completed and following the Board of Trade inspection opened to Cirencester 31 May 1841, worked by the GWR. Thousands attended the opening and 'Many were afraid to approach the engine, but anxious to obtain a full insight as to its construction, fixed themselves in some conspicuous and prominent part to view this surprising affair, until every bridge or eminence whether over the deep cutting or on the raised ground was literally covered with observers and their curiosity was amply gratified.' On 1 July 1843 the GWR took over the CGWUR and for £230,000 acquired works which had cost £600,000.

Meanwhile it was agreed that the Bristol & Gloucester Railway would share the line between Standish and Gloucester. As the impecunious CGWUR when pressed by the BGR was naturally chary at giving a completion date, it was decided that the BGR would lay the Standish to Gloucester section and offer running powers to the CGWUR. Although in 1837 preliminary shafts were sunk for Sapperton Tunnel, work did not begin in earnest until 1839. Richard Boxall, a former pupil of the architect Augustus Pugin, was appointed resident engineer.

Several accidents were recorded. On 15 September 1844 George Freeman aged 26 and Henry Stokes, 33, were working below 'an immense mass of stone two or three tons in weight' engaged in boring a hole to insert powder for blasting, when the rock fell and killed them. Four days later Edward Harratt was crushed when three tons of earth fell on him. Dug out, he died the following day.

The line opened from Kemble to Gloucester on 12 May 1845 just to passengers. At Gloucester the GWR used a platform on the north side of the Birmingham & Gloucester terminus and which had been used

Kemble, view Up circa 1960. Despite the 'Cirencester Town' blind, the rail bus stands at the Tetbury platform. Author's collection

by BGR trains since the previous July. Brimscombe and Stonehouse stations opened 1 June 1845 and Gloucester and Stroud opened to goods 15 September 1845.

In May 1902 a US citizen, Thomas Nevins, who four years earlier had formed a company for laying electric tramways in Cheltenham, proposed the Stroud District Tramways Company. Lines were to radiate from Stroud to Chalford, Nailsworth, Stonehouse, Painswick, Gloucester and Cheltenham. The Light Railway Commissioners failed to grant an order as the tramways would have competed with the GWR and MR.

As stations in the industrialised Golden Valley between Stroud and Chalford were too far apart to be of much use to mill and factory workers, the GWR felt that a fresh tramway application might prove successful. It had learnt its lesson when the opening of the Camborne & Redruth Tramway reduced rail passengers between these stations from 33,973 in 1901 to 7,859 in 1902.

A GWR report of 20 April 1903 proposed operating an hourly service 6.00am to 10.00pm with halts being opened at level crossings. Fares would be ½ d a mile with a minimum fare of 1d. The service would be operated by steam rail motors – a passenger coach and locomotive on one under frame. Capable of being driven from either end, it obviated the need to run an engine round at the end of each journey.

In the spring of 1903 when it was building its own rail motors, the GWR managed to borrow the London & South Western and London, Brighton & South Coast Railways Joint Committee railcar No 2 over the weekend of 9/10 May 1903.

Designed for the 1¼ mile long Fratton to East Southsea branch, it was found unsuited to the Stroud Valley, as with a load of 30 passengers, speed on the 1 in 70 gradient between Brimscombe and Chalford did not exceed 8mph and it only reached 27mph on the level. Churchward, the GWR's Chief Mechanical Engineer, witnessed the trial and was confident that the GWR rail motor would not encounter this problem.

The new service started between Chalford and Stonehouse 12 October 1903, tickets issued tramway-style by a conductor on the train. The service was worked by one car, with a second held in reserve. About 5,000 passengers were carried on the first Saturday, the two cars working coupled together. These rail motors became so popular that in 1905, for three months the GWR augmented the rail motor service with motor buses until further rail motors were available.

Experience proved that rail motors were not really satisfactory as if a trailer was added at a busy time, difficulty was experienced climbing gradients and the schedule could not be kept. The machinery was removed from the motors to convert them into trailers which were alternately pull and pushed by 0-6-0ST, 0-6-0PT or 0-4-2Ts. These locomotives were adapted so they could be controlled when pushing by a driver in the control compartment at the end of an auto trailer.

In 1921 the service was regularly extended from Stonehouse to Gloucester and the last rail motor in the Golden Valley ran in July 1928. The auto trains were withdrawn 2 November 1964 – the last such service on the Western Region.

The CGWUR entered Gloucestershire just south of the 415yd long Kemble Tunnel. On 28 July 1968 the line from Swindon to Kemble was singled, but at the time of writing, is being doubled again.

At first Kemble was merely a junction for changing to or from the Cirencester branch, as Squire Gordon would not permit a public station on his land. The present station of Tudor design was opened 1 May 1882. It still remains open and enjoys busy commuter traffic. The water supply to Swindon Locomotive Works was augmented by running water trains from Kemble, but by the early nineteen-hundreds, a more efficient method was required. A new pump house was built and a pipeline laid to Swindon. As a burst water main could have washed away an embankment, for safety a 'Burst Pipe' indicator was fitted in Kemble signal box and if it gave a warning, a light engine was sent to inspect the track.

A mile north of Kemble station was Tetbury Road, closed to passengers when the new Kemble station opened, but being retained for goods until 1 July 1963. To avoid confusion with Tetbury itself, on 1 May 1908 it was renamed Coates.

Sapperton Sidings signal box as well as the main line, controlled Up and Down loops until closure 5 October 1970. Beyond the line enters the 352yd long Sapperton Short Tunnel, followed by a break of 66yd in the summit cutting before plunging into the 1,864yd Sapperton Long Tunnel. Ten shafts were opened to make the tunnel, but only two remain open for ventilation.

Coates goods station, 1934, view Up. Author's collection

The line emerges from the tunnel above the Golden Valley, in steam train days a Stop Board required Down freight trains to halt and pin down brakes. As the line has a series of reverse curves, all traffic was limited to a speed of 40mph.

No 4028 *The Roumanian Monarch* heading an Up express emerges from the eastern portal of the Long Sapperton Tunnel. M.J.Tozer collection

2884 class 2-8-0 No 2896 climbs to Sapperton Tunnel 7 May 1955 assisted in the rear by 43XX class 2-6-0 No 6354. The author can be seen on the right in the mid-distance. R.E.Toop

The 129yd long 12 span Frampton Viaduct was originally of timber as were the others. Some of the timbers remain encased in brick. By milepost 97 is an unusually steep occupation bridge carrying a footpath on a gradient of 1 in 2.9. The 320yd long Chalford Viaduct is unusual in that due to steeply sloping ground, it is one sided.

Chalford station opened 2 August 1897 and was the terminus of the rail motor and auto train services. A rail motor shed was provided but early on 10 January 1916, just after midnight the shed caught fire. Signalman Harry Grimmett was roused, ran to his closed signal box and telephoned Brimscombe for assistance. The shed and rail motor No 48 were destroyed, but two trailers and a gas tank wagon used for charging the lights, were

Chalford circa 1905. Behind the station building is a cattle pen. Author's collection

removed to safety. It was never rebuilt, so although rail motors or tank engines were sub-shedded at Chalford for a further 35 years, they were left in the open. The 'shed' closed and locomotives and staff were transferred to Brimscombe 21 May 1951.

The single span 74ft St Mary's Viaduct crossed the Thames & Severn Canal and beyond, St Mary's Crossing Halt opened 12 October 1903 and closed, like others on the line, 2 November 1964.

Brimscombe opened 1 June 1845, was a neat Brunelian station. It was provided with a shed to house banking engines to assist trains up Sapperton bank which has gradients as steep as 1 in 60. The shed closed 28 October 1963 when bankers were sent out daily from Gloucester until 6 March 1965

14XX class 0-4-2T No 1453 with a home-made smoke box number plate, enters Brimscombe with a Gloucester to Chalford auto train 13 April 1964. Rev. Alan Newman

14xx Class 0-4-2T No 1453 propels a Chalford to Gloucester auto train and diesel-hydraulic D7031 heads an Up train at Brimscombe, 13 April 1964. Rev. Alan Newman

A nineteen-thirties trade card depicts the GW & LMS railways joint delivery 3 ton Scammell 3-wheel mechanical horse based at Stroud. It only hauled one trailer at a time. Author's collection

4-6-0 No 7815 *Fritwell Manor* awaiting a banking turn as 14XX class 0-4-2T No 1458 accelerates from Brimscombe station with a Gloucester to Chalford auto train 25 August 1964. Notice that the water tank forms the shed roof and above the entrance, a duct carries away fumes from the interior. Rev. Alan Newman

when the use of diesel power reduced the requirement. Brimscombe station closed to goods 12 August 1963 and passengers 2 November 1964.

Beyond is the 168yd long Bourne Viaduct over the canal. Brimscombe Bridge Halt opened 1 February 1904, its platforms staggered each side of the bridge. Ham Mill Crossing Halt opened 12 October 1903; Bowbridge Crossing Halt 1 May 1905 and immediately preceding Stroud station is Capel's Viaduct, 253yd followed by the Canal Viaduct of a single span over the Stroudwater Canal and three other spans.

Brimscombe Bridge Halt 9 October 1950. The tunnel beyond the bridge is only about 3yd in length. Author's collection

Stroud station remains open. With the vast increase of traffic following the introduction of the rail motor service, its platforms became crowded. The buildings on the Down side were demolished, new ones built set back and both platforms lengthened. Watt's Viaduct, 132yd and Stratford Viaduct, 73yd, are west of the station. Downfield Crossing Halt opened 12 October 1903 and beyond is Carpenter's Viaduct, 47yds. Cashes Green Halt opened

64XX class 0-6-0PT No 6437 heading the 10.45am Gloucester to Chalford takes on water at Stroud, 24 April 1962. Author

21 January 1930 and Ebley Crossing Halt 12 October 1903. Jefferies' Siding opened 26 July 1898 to serve a brickworks. The original buildings at Stonehouse were demolished and a new building opened in 1977.

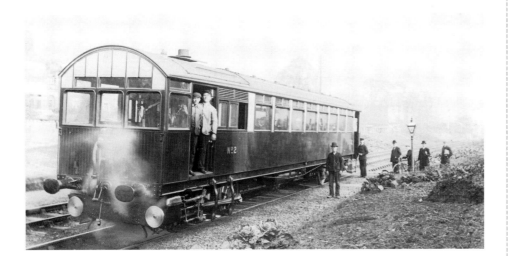

T. Cratchley's advertisement in the *Stroud Journal* 27 February 1886.

Steam rail motor No 2 at Ebley Crossing Halt in its early days when merely a stopping place with no platform. Author's collection

Steam rail motor No 50 at Ebley Crossing Halte – note the early spelling. Author's collection

Stonehouse
(Burdett Road),
view Up circa 1963.
Lens of Sutton

Standish Junction is where the BGR and the CGWUR met and ran parallel to Gloucester. It first opened 8 July 1844, but closed 19 May 1854 when the MR opened its independent standard gauge line. Following the abolition of broad gauge in the Gloucester area, the junction was reinstated 21 April 1873. As part of rationalisation of lines in the Gloucester area, the four tracks Gloucester to Standish were reduced to two.

The CGWUR station at Gloucester was on the site of the present station. The South Wales line station originally had two platforms, but by 1855 the up platform was removed to free its site for sidings. The former Down platform was lengthened in order to be used for trains from both directions and absorbed the site of the former CGWUR terminus. A new Up platform was built in 1899. When the former MR station, Eastgate, was closed 1 December 1975, all traffic was concentrated on a rebuilt Central station, traffic again using one long platform, lengthened to 1,600ft and being the second longest in the country.

Gloucester view Up
circa 1850. George
Measom

Brand-new Star class 4-6-0 No 4023 *King George* heads the Royal Train at Gloucester 23 June 1909. A Royal Train carries four headlamps. The coach on the right is a 4-wheeler. Author's collection

Transferring from broad gauge to standard gauge at Gloucester: even the dog thinks it's a nuisance.
Courtesy: Illustrated London News

Gloucester T station house 1 April 1954. Passengers from Gloucester would have stepped out of their coach in front of the two windows, left, after crossing at right-angles the line in the foreground. Dr A.J.G. Dickens

7 GWR Main Lines: The South Wales Railway

ALTHOUGH THE line between Gloucester and Chepstow was virtually one railway, it was actually built by two companies. The 7½ miles Gloucester to Grange Court was built by the Gloucester & Dean Forest Railway (GDFR)whose Act received Royal Assent 27 July 1846, while the remaining 19 miles were constructed by the South Wales Railway (SWR) which received its Act on the same date to lay a line to Grange Court Junction.

Work began on the GDFR in 1847, but in the aftermath following the Railway Mania, investors were loath to risk their money in railways, so a shortage of funds caused construction works to be suspended for two years. The bridge at Over was completed in August 1850, but the bridge nearer Gloucester was not ready until the following year. Although navigation on this stretch of the river had been blocked by the old stone bridge further

A Down South Wales Railway train heads away from Gloucester through the floods November 1852. Author's collection

downstream, the Lords of the Admiralty at the instigation of the Severn Improvement Commissioners, had a clause inserted in the company's Act forcing the railway to make an opening bridge in case the road bridge was ever altered.

Brunel, the company's engineer, designed a skew bridge capable of turning on a central pier formed of five cast iron columns filled with concrete. The construction of this bridge delayed the opening of the line.

The completed GDFR was leased to the GWR at the rate of 4½ per cent on its capital and this was raised to 5½ per cent with the opening of the line to Hereford. This little line proved to be a good investment and maintained a nominal existence until 1875 when was taken over by the GWR.

In 1844 when the SWR was originally planned, it was proposed to leave the CGWUR at Standish and cross the Severn between Fretherne and Awre. However this plan was scotched when the Admiralty used its veto against such a bridge

By August 1837 work had started on the Chepstow to Grange Court section of the SWR, but then that company, like the GDFR found difficulty in raising money. Eventually the line was built and on 19 September 1851 trains were able to steam from Gloucester to a temporary station called Chepstow East, situated at the road bridge close to what was to become the junction of the Wye Valley branch and situated about a mile east of Chepstow station. Passengers were conveyed by horse buses between the two stations each side of the Wye. There was, of course, scarcely any through goods traffic due to transhipment difficulties. Intermediate stations were at Oakle Street, Newnham and Lydney.

To conclude the story, one track over the Wye Bridge was opened 19 July 1852, exactly ten months after the opening of the line to Gloucester. This

4-6-0 5010 *Restormel Castle* has crossed Chepstow Bridge into Gloucestershire. 'SW' indicates 'Sound whistle'. Author's collection

completed through rail communication between London and Swansea, reducing the time to five hours from the 15 hours needed when travelling by train, then boat across the Beachley to Aust ferry and then coach. The opening of the line brought the lease of the SWR by the GWR into force. The line was managed by a joint committee of five directors from each company. The GWR provided locomotives and rolling stock, while the SWR offered accommodation for traffic. The SWR was finally amalgamated with the GWR in 1863. In the eighteen-fifties and sixties Messrs Hennessey & Son, Swansea, sent an employee every Monday to wind clocks at SWR stations. At every station a porter was ordered to have a ladder ready and waiting by the clock so that the horologist could ascend, wind the instrument and adjust its hands. If necessary the train was kept waiting in order that he could do the journey in a day. If a clock had problems, he made a special journey and replaced it.

Gloucester to Grange Court was converted to mixed gauge 20 August 1869 and Grange Court to Cardiff to standard gauge 11 May 1872.

A broad gauge conversion staff train at Grange Court, May 1872. Notice the men standing on the disc and crossbar signals. The track is cross-sleepered. Author's collection

West of the GWR Gloucester station, the branch from Llanthony Docks trailed in. This line opened 20 March 1854 and en route, bridged the Severn. Regular traffic ceased early in 1989. At Over Junction the branch to Ledbury (see page 124) left and beyond were the extensive Over Sidings, taken out of use in 1969.

Oakle Street, besides having a curious name for a settlement, unusually had no canopy in front of the main building. It closed to passengers, as did the other stations on the line, 2 November 1964. Grange Court was an isolated four platformed station serving a small rural community. The station was rebuilt in 1855 for the opening of the Hereford, Ross & Gloucester Railway. Westbury on Severn Halt opened 9 July 1928, closed 10 August 1959.

Newnham, originally with two platforms, had a Down bay platform added 4 August 1907 for Cinderford branch trains. It later saw little use as trains for Cinderford normally ran through from Gloucester. Beyond the station is a 232yd long tunnel. Ruddle Road Halt, with staggered platforms,

Grange Court Junction, view Up August 1963. Part of the Up platform has been re-planked. S. Apperley

In August 1907 2021 class 0-6-0ST No 2062 at Newnham heads a push-pull train to Steam Mills. The bay platform was opened 4 August 1907 especially for this service. Author's collection

opened 3 August 1907 with the Newnham to Steam Mills Crossing halt passenger service. Little-used, it closed 30 April 1917.

A sizeable yard was provided at Bullo Pill to deal with traffic to and from the Cinderford branch and also the line to Bullo Pill basin and quay. The line was cut back to the basin 4 August 1907 and the basin line closed 26 June 1949. The main line crossed the 40yd long Bullo Pill Viaduct to Awre for Blakeney. From 25 May 1868 it was the junction for the goods-only Forest of Dean Central Railway. The station closed to passengers and goods 10

August 1959. The Forest of Dean Central Railway closed to traffic 29 July 1949, but was used until 1961 for wagon storage.

Lydney is now only a shadow of its past and although still open, the GWR buildings have been demolished and replaced by basic shelters. Immediately west of the station the Severn & Wye Railway crossed on its way to Lydney Docks. East of the station was a large nest of exchange sidings, many taken out of use by 1969. From the Down loop a private siding agreement dated 28 May 1941 gave access to the Ministry of Supply's Lydney Salvage Depot. Taken over by Lydney Industrial Holdings Limited, a new agreement of 8 August 1961 was made, but terminated about March 1964.

Awre for Blakeney circa 1910. Author's collection

Woolaston closed to passengers and goods 1 December 1954. Unlike most stations, as opposed to halts, until 1902 it lacked a goods siding. A shipyard workers' platform was established at Beachley 18 November 1918 until 3 March 1919. Extensive lines served the National Shipyard opened about 1917, but following the Armistice the yard closed in 1919. At Wye Valley Junction the branch from Monmouth trailed in and immediately beyond was Tutshill Halt, opened 9 July 1934 and closed 5 January 1959. The line crosses the Wye Bridge into Gwent.

43XX 2-6-0 No 5398 heads an Up freight through Lydney Junction 14 June 1958. R.E.Toop

8 GWR Main Lines: Badminton to the Severn Tunnel, Bristol to the Severn Tunnel, The Severn Tunnel

Badminton to the Severn Tunnel

DURING THE latter half of the nineteenth century people often jokingly said that the initials 'GWR' stood for 'Great Way Round' and certainly many of the Great Western's main lines were far from being direct.

When the Severn Tunnel was first used by passenger trains in 1886, expresses from London to South Wales had to curve southwards at Wootton Bassett, pass through Bath and Bristol and then bear northwards again to reach the tunnel. Trains were obviously running an unnecessary mileage and a direct line was needed through the southern end of the Cotswolds between Wootton Bassett and Filton, north of Bristol.

James C. Inglis, chief engineer of the GWR, piloted the Bristol & South Wales Direct Railway (BSWDR) bill with such skill that no opposition was encountered in the Parliamentary Committee stage. The estimated cost of the 33½ miles of line was £1,300,000. The Act was passed on 7 August 1896 and the contract for construction let to S. Pearson & Son early the following year.

The undertaking was the biggest of the kind to be carried out after the extension of the Great Central Railway to London a few years before. The contactor's plant consisted of 75 miles of temporary lines; 50 locomotives; 17 steam navvies; 11 steam cranes; 1,800 earth wagons and three large brickworks. More than 4,000 men were employed. 50 million bricks and 20,000 tons of cement and lime were used.

The line was laid for speedy running, no gradient being steeper than 1 in

300 and no curve sharper than one mile radius. Considering that the line had to cross the Cotswold Hills, this was a fine achievement. Four of the stations had quadruple track enabling non-stop trains to by-pass the platforms, and, if necessary, overtake slower ones. Most of the embankments were wide enough to allow for quadrupling throughout and the length of the two tunnels totalled nearly three miles; the three viaducts had a total of 28 arches, while in addition were 88 bridges.

The first section of the line to be opened was from Wootton Bassett to Badminton on 1 January 1903, but only for goods traffic. The first through goods train to use the whole of the line left Bristol at 8.30 am on 1 May 1903. The first passenger train, the 6.32 am, used the line two months later on 1 July. It carried the superintendent of the Bristol Division of the GWR and several company officials, but there was no special opening ceremony, though children at most schools along the line were given a holiday. Four new direct expresses from Paddington to South Wales were run over the line.

A Down stopping train calls at Badminton circa 1903. The tank engine, left, may be shunting the goods yard. Author's collection

The BSWDR may well have been used to break a speed record. In May 1906, No 2903 *Lady of Lyons* proved that a newly-built locomotive could achieve 100 mph without causing mechanical harm. It was the practice to send new engines on trial trips from Swindon to Stoke Gifford and back. No 2903 was held at Chipping Sodbury until the line was clear to Wootton Bassett. At last the signal fell and the driver gave the engine her head. The timing for some distance by the quarter mileposts was given as 120 mph, thus antedating the exploits of today's High Speed Trains by 70 years.

The first part of the BSWDR is in Wiltshire, but it crosses into Gloucestershire just before Badminton. A unique feature of this station was a limestone plaque at the west end of the building on the Up side displaying the coat of arms of the Duke of Beaufort, an important landowner. The Beaufort Hunt provided traffic during the season, as before the days of road transport, a hound van was based at the station and added to a rake of horse boxes and passenger coaches.

As part of the agreement by which the GWR was allowed to construct the line through the Beaufort Estate, four passenger trains in each direction were required to call daily and additionally, any train had to call if a first class passenger wished to alight. In 1913 an average of 40 passengers a day, including Sundays, used Badminton station. Circa 1960 the numbers of first and second class tickets issued was approximately equal. One lady travelled first class from Badminton to London just to purchase a pair of shoes. The station closed to goods 1 November 1966 and passengers 3 June 1968, over seven years later than the other stations on the line which lost their passenger services 3 April 1961.

Goods wagons stand on the Down Through Road at Badminton circa 1903. Author's collection

GWR AEC lorry No 755, XT 6394 at Badminton February 1928, with a load of old-style milk churns. Notice the lack of windscreen, but a tarpaulin is provided to partly shelter driver and mate in inclement weather. A radiator muff is fitted and the headlamp is fuelled by acetylene gas. Author's collection

Following closure of these stations, the travelling safe into which the daily takings from Badminton were placed, was sent to Paddington, instead of Bristol, on the first morning train, the cash bag inside sealed with a brass padlock. It was returned empty on the first available train from Paddington. Unloading the safe took time and while the Badminton porter was doing this, he was unable to assist passengers. Gerald Fiennes, area manager, stopped this practice and takings were henceforth paid into a Yate bank, Badminton then being under the care of Yate station.

West of Badminton is the 4,444 yd long Chipping Sodbury Tunnel which has suffered flooding problems over the years. The line was closed 2–20 August 2004 in order to carry out remedial work. West of the tunnel were 524 yd long water troughs set between the rails 29 June 1906 so that

A permanent way pump trolley at the east end of Sodbury Tunnel. A ventilating shaft can be seen towards the top of the picture. Author's collection

locomotives could pick up water without stopping. Water was taken from a stream at the east end of Sodbury Tunnel. The troughs were spanned by an aqueduct carrying the River Frome in a 95 ft long steel trough. The railway dipped beneath it and this dip also tended to become flooded. In 1986 giant jacks lifted the aqueduct and the banks on the upstream side were also raised. The track was then lifted to remove the dip.

4-6-0 No 7909 *Heveningham Hall* with a Down goods on Sodbury water troughs 15 June 1962. An aqueduct is above. The west portal of Sodbury Tunnel can just be seen. Author

Wapley Common Depot opened in 1943 and the private siding agreement terminated 31 May 1967. The contractors laying the siding hired GWR locomotive No 5, an ex- London, Brighton & South Coast Railway Terrier 0-6-0T which it had obtained from the closed Weston, Clevedon & Portishead Railway. No 5 was, at one time, on loan to the nearby Coalpit Heath Colliery. Initially the two vast storage sheds at Wapley Common were

for US military equipment, but later used for Royal Naval stores. In the post war period, Celestine from a quarry at Yate, and used to make perfume, was despatched by rail. Wagons which carried it required careful sweeping out and the signalman at Wapley Common was paid overtime to carry out this task. The wagons were then taken from Wapley Common Sidings to the dock at Chipping Sodbury for loading.

Just beyond Wapley Common was Westerleigh triangular junction giving access to and from the LMS Yate to Gloucester line over which the GWR had running powers. The east curve of the triangle has had a chequered history being opened and closed several times, final closure coming 4 January 1950.

A Down goods is held at Chipping Sodbury station for a train behind it to pass. Two horse boxes stand in the dock siding, right. Workmen repair the platform edging. Author's collection

An Up express hauled by a Western class diesel-hydraulic passes Coalpit Heath on the through road, circa 1966. It is after closure to passengers, as the platform canopy has been removed. Author's collection

The BSWDR crossed the LMS Bristol to Gloucester railway and a colliery line and just before Coalpit Heath station, a line to the colliery branched off. The 95 yd long Coalpit Heath Viaduct is crossed and when built, one buttress descended into the coal mine. The 269 yd long Hackford Viaduct is just prior to the double-track Winterbourne station. Beyond the 139 yd Winterbourne Viaduct was Stoke Gifford, one of Bristol's principal goods yards, with 14 sidings on the Up side and 10 on the Down.

Bristol Parkway passenger station opened on the site 1 May 1972, since when many of the sidings have been lifted. The Parkway station was a new concept to capture motorists. It allowed people living on the north side of Bristol an opportunity to use trains without having to reach Temple Meads. It was also convenient for Bath people travelling northwards who, by using the station, avoided changing trains at Temple Meads. Trains on the Paddington to South Wales route and Bristol to Birmingham both called. Initially the 600 space car park was free and proved so popular that it was increased to 1,000 spaces. It is said that today, Parkway station has higher receipts than Temple Meads as most of its ticket sales are for long journeys. West of Parkway, lines to Bristol, Avonmouth and the Severn Tunnel divide.

In preparation for running High Speed Trains over the line, from Wootton Bassett to Parkway, the track required blanketing with sand and polythene sheeting to restore good drainage. The option was offered of either three years of disruption under a series of weekend possession, or complete closure for five months. The latter was chosen and work proceeded round the clock during the summer of 1975.

Bristol to the Severn Tunnel

Early in 1854 there was a proposal to build a railway from Bristol via Shirehampton to New Passage with a floating bridge across the Severn. This idea came to naught, but the Bristol & South Wales Union Railway (BSWUR) Act received Royal Assent 27 July 1857 to build 11½ miles of broad gauge line from South Wales Junction, a quarter of a mile east of Temple Meads, to

New Passage Pier, whence a ferry would run to Portskewett Pier the other side of the Severn, a distance of two miles. Construction commenced in October 1858 and the following year the two ferries were again purchased.

The ceremonial opening of New Passage Pier & Railway 25 August 1863. Author's collection

When Brunel invited Charles Richardson to be resident engineer on the BSWUR he wrote: 'I want a man acquainted with tunnelling and who will, with a moderate amount of inspecting assistance, look after the Tunnel [Patchway] with his own eyes, for I am beginning to be sick of Inspectors who see nothing, and resident engineers who reside at home...The country immediately north of Bristol I should think a delightful one to live in – beautiful country – good society near Bristol and Clifton etc. I can't vouch for any cricketing, but I should think it highly probable.' Richardson was offered an annual salary of £300-450.

The piers designed by Charles Richardson were of timber on a stone base. Trains ran to the end of the pier, and stairs and steam-operated lifts took passengers to pontoons consisting of hulks moored alongside allowing ferry steamers to berth at all states of the tide, despite a rise of as much as 46ft. Over the pier head and for some distance along the platforms, was a roof of corrugated iron. The pier was 1,635ft in length. It had its own hotel and private gas works.

The line opened on 8 September 1863 and was worked by the GWR under an agreement dated 17 February 1864 and formally amalgamated with it at par on 1 August 1868. The line was converted to standard gauge between 7 and 9 August 1873, and at the latter date, South Wales Junction, Bristol to Narroways Hill was double tracked. Narroways Hill Junction to Patchway was doubled by laying a new Up line which was brought into use on 1 September 1886, the day the Severn Tunnel was open to goods trains. The tunnel was opened to passenger trains on 1 December 1886 together with the High Level station at Pilning.

The Bristol end of the Severn Tunnel. On the left a workman is using a grindstone to sharpen a tool. Author's collection

The original Filton station was situated immediately south of today's bridge over the A4174 Ring Road. This first station closed 1 July 1903 and replaced by a new four-platformed station 200yd north. Opened 1 July 1903 it was renamed Filton Junction 9 May 1910. This station closed 8 March 1996, being replaced by Filton Abbey Wood a little to the south and, apart from local residents, is used by employees of the Ministry of Defence and those attending the University of the West of England.

The original Patchway station closed 10 August 1885 and was replaced on this date by one a quarter of a mile to the south. This was necessary, as when the line was doubled, the gradient of the new line, which became the Up, was on an easier gradient and at the site of the original station, the two lines were on different levels. The original line (which became the Down) had two tunnels, 1,246yd and 66yd respectively, while the new Up line opened 27 May 1887 had one tunnel 1,756yd.

The original Pilning station was at a lower level than that on today's main line. The second Pilning station opened 1 December 1886. Before the opening of the Severn Bridge car trains were run for passengers wishing to avoid the Aust-Beachley Ferry. The special train consisted of a passenger coach and flat wagons for vehicles. Although Pilning station is still open today it is only served by one train in each direction.

72XX class 2-8-2T No 7233 and No 7250 double-head a Down freight through Patchway 6 August 1963. It was rare to see two engines of this class coupled together. E.T.Gill courtesy Rev. Brian Arman

Star Class 4-6-0 No 4044 *Prince George* climbs to Patchway 26 April 1936 with a north to west express comprising at least 13 vehicles. The siding on the right is level; the Down line, left, when out of the picture descends at 1 in 68, whereas the Up line which the express is climbing, is at a steady 1 in 100. Author's collection

5101 class 2-6-2T No 4136 (86E Severn Tunnel Junction) at Pilning 21 March 1963 with a train of car flats. Rev. Alan Newman

153333 working the 07.42 Cardiff Central to Weymouth calls at Pilning 20 August 1990. It is the only Up train to use the station. Author

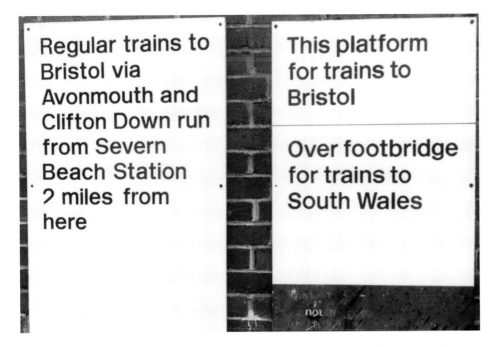

Regular trains to Bristol via Avonmouth and Clifton Down run from Severn Beach Station 2 miles from here

This platform for trains to Bristol

Over footbridge for trains to South Wales

Notices at Pilning 16 July 1990. It is unusual for a station to suggest passengers use another station. The word 'Trains' on the right-hand notice would be better in the singular, as but one train runs daily in each direction. Author

The line to New Passage Pier became redundant when the Severn Tunnel opened, so was closed 1 December 1886. Immediately prior to closing, the pier was served by eight trains each way daily on weekdays and two on Sundays. Additionally there was a local passenger and goods station on the landward end of the pier at which all passenger trains and two daily freight trains called.

A new single line almost 7¾ miles long was built from Avonmouth to Pilning, running close to the Severn and joining the site of the original Bristol & South Wales Union Railway near New Passage and utilising its trackbed for 1¾ miles. Its opening on 5 February 1900 shortened the route for goods traffic from Avonmouth to South Wales and avoided the congestion at Bristol. The first train traversed the line at 7.00pm – unusually late in the day for an inauguration. On 23 June 1928 the branch was adapted for passenger traffic with a station at Severn Beach, then a newly-made river resort, and halts opened at New Passage, Cross Hands and Pilning on 9 July 1928.

On 9 May 1910 a new direct line, 6¾ miles long was opened from Holesmouth Junction near Avonmouth, to Filton Junction and Stoke Gifford. This provided a new outlet for up country traffic and avoided the use of the heavily graded Clifton line. Towards the end of 1916, the construction of what would have been the second largest government factory in the

Notice advising staff of the opening of New Passage & Cross Hands Halts.

Private and not for Publication.   Notice No. S.1344.

GREAT WESTERN RAILWAY.
(For the use of Company's Servants only.)

Opening of New Passenger Halts
AT
NEW PASSAGE & CROSS HANDS
AND
New Passenger Platform at PILNING (Low Level)

On **Monday, July 9th, 1928**, new Passenger Platforms 150 feet in length, situated at Pilning (Low Level), Cross Hands, and New Passage, between Severn Beach and Pilning Junction, will be opened. Passenger traffic only will be dealt with at Cross Hands and New Passage. Passenger traffic and parcels traffic will be dealt with at Pilning (Low Level).

Tickets will not be issued at Cross Hands and New Passage Halts, but by the G.W.R. Agents. Mr. W. Boon for New Passage and Mrs. Humphries, Cross Hands.

Tickets from Pilning (Low Level) Platform will be issued at Pilning (High Level).

FARES FROM HALTS.

TO (Via Patchway.)	Third Single from: New Passage.	Cross Hands.	Pilning (L.L.)	TO	Third Single from: New Passage.	Cross Hands.	Pilning (L.L.),
	s. d.	s. d.	s. d.		s. d.	s. d.	s. d.
Bristol (Tem. Meads)	1 5	1 4	1 3	Bristol (Tem. Meads)	1 5	1 4	—
Lawrence Hill	1 3	1 3	1 1	Lawrence Hill	1 3	1 3	—
Bristol (Stap. Rd.)	1 3	1 2	1 0	Bristol (Stap. Rd.)	1 3	1 2	—
Montpelier	1 4	1 3	1 2	Montpelier	1 6	1 7	—
Redland	1 5	1 4	1 3	Redland	1 6	1 6	—
Clifton Down	1 6	1 5	—	Clifton Down	1 5	1 6	—
Ashley Hill	1 1	1 0	0 10½	Sea Mills	1 2	1 3	1 3
Horfield	0 11½	0 10½	0 9	Shirehampton	0 10½	0 11½	1 1
Filton Junction	0 10	0 9	0 7½	Avonmouth Dock	0 9	0 9	0 11
North Filton	0 10½	0 10	—	St. Andrew's Road	0 7½	0 8½	0 9
Henbury	1 3	1 2	—	Severn Beach	0 2½	0 4	0 4
Bath	2 9	2 8	2 6	New Passage	—	0 1½	0 2½
				Cross Hands	0 1½	—	0 1½

(Right-hand section headed "Via Severn Beach.")

Return Journey Fares Double Single Fares.

Cheap day tickets (available on day of issue only) will be issued by certain trains daily from and to stations in Bristol district.

Cheap tickets from the Halts must be obtained from the Agents before commencing the journey, otherwise ordinary fares must be collected.

For particulars of the trains by which these tickets are available and fares see public announcements.

As the platforms will not accommodate a complete train, but only two coaches, passengers for the Halts must be confined to the two rear coaches, and in drawing up at the Halts care must be taken that these coaches are stopped alongside platform.

New Passage Halt will be under the supervision of the Severn Beach Station Master. Pilning (Low Level) Platform and Cross Hands Halt will be under the supervision of Pilning Station Master.

Guards must take notice of passengers joining trains with bicycles, mail carts, dogs, etc., from the halts and must draw the attention of the staff at the next station to such passengers so that the necessary charges can be collected.

Guards of trains calling at Cross Hands and New Passage must collect tickets from passengers alighting there, and hand same to the person in charge at Pilning (Low Level) in the case of Up trains, to the person in charge at Severn Beach in the case of Down trains.

To ensure passengers travelling in the last two coaches, and to avoid passengers alighting at Halts without tickets, care must be taken by Station Staff and Guards that passengers travelling to the Halts enter these coaches and are in possession of tickets.

Lighting.—The Station Masters at Pilning and Severn Beach will arrange for the trimming and lighting of the lamps at Cross Hands and New Passage respectively, and the Guard of the last train stopping at the Halts will extinguish the lights.

H. R. GRIFFITHS,
Divisional Superintendent.

Bristol, July, 1928.
(500 R. 8vo.)   †J. W. Arrowsmith Ltd., Printers, Quay Street, Bristol.

country was started at Chittening and the provision of sidings and the doubling of the line was carried out by 13 May 1917, but the entry of the USA into the war caused the government to abandon this project. A new station was opened on 13 November 1918 and closed 11 October 1923. Following the outbreak of WW2 there was an unadvertised opening of the platform 27 October 1941. It closed 1 August 1946, only to re-open for workmen 25 August 1947. The official public opening occurred on 31 May 1948, only to close finally 23 November 1964, when the passenger service on the line was withdrawn. Hallen Halt also had a varied history. Opened with the new line on 9 May 1910, as a wartime economy measure, it closed 22 March 1915 and then on 10 March 1917 reopened unadvertised on a site a short distance west of the original to serve workers at a nearby government factory. It closed finally October 1918.

Fireman's view from a Class 8F 2-8-0 of Hallen Marsh Junction, March 1964. The Henbury line curves right and the Severn Beach line is straight ahead. W.F. Grainger

Henbury station had standard GWR red brick buildings and an unusual feature was a goldfish pond on the platform. As a WW1 economy measure it closed to the public on 22 March 1915, but continued to be used by unadvertised workmen's services, over 6,000 passengers using it daily. With track doubling, an Up platform was brought into use 27 May 1917. The station reopened to the public 10 July 1922. It closed to passengers 23 November 1964. Charlton Halt was the only one on the line with a simple history: it opened 9 May 1910 and closed 22 March 1915. Beyond the halt the line enters the 302yd long Charlton Tunnel. To the east the 90ft wide Bristol Aircraft Corporation level crossing was opened 15 November 1948 to accommodate the runway requirements of the large Brabazon airliner. Filton Halt opened with a 150ft long platform 9 May 1910 and closed 22

March 1915; it then reopened 12 July 1926 with 350ft platforms – the track had been doubled in the interim. In 1940 the platforms were extended to 640ft. It closed to the public 23 November 1964, but remained open for workmen's services until 12 May 1986. Beyond is the Filton Junctions complex offering routes to the Severn Tunnel, Bristol Parkway and Temple Meads. The Hallen Marsh Junction to Filton line was doubled 1917, singled 1964-66 and then doubled in the summer of 1992 to deal with the merry-go-round coal trains from Avonmouth to Didcot and Aberthaw power stations.

Fireman's view of Henbury, as a Class 9 2-10-0 passes through in October 1963.
W.F.Grainger

Charlton Halt, view Up. Preparations have been made for doubling. Author's collection

Returning to Hallen Marsh Junction, the single line continues northwards parallel with the coast to Severn Beach. This opened 5 June 1922 as an excursion platform only and then fully 26 May 1924. In 1938 an attempt was made to popularise the resort and for the first time through excursions were run from Redditch, Great Malvern, Birmingham and Gloucester. LMS engines worked these trains as far as Avonmouth Dock.

Charlton Tunnel view Up from a Class 8F 2-8-0, March 1964 in double track days. The distant signal above the smoke box is for Filton West. W.F.Grainger

North Filton Platform circa 1962: Filton West Junction is beyond the bridge and carriage sidings to the left. At the top of the slope is the ticket hut. Lens of Sutton

The power-operated gates of the Bristol Aeroplane Company's crossing, 21 August 1980. Author

The Bristol to South Wales line crosses the Avonmouth to Badminton line. On the left are Filton West carriage sidings brought into use 27 July 1942 and removed 1968.
W.F.Grainger

Beyond Severn Beach, on the east side of the line a semi-circular bank marked the entrance to the Severn Tunnel. On the other side a trailing siding led to the pumping station and the smell of tunnel mustiness pervaded the whole area. The Sea Wall Pumping Station Siding was taken out of use 27 October 1963. The local goods train, called the 'Bricky' as it called at Cattybrook Brick Works, delivered coal for the pumps approximately weekly. The line curved to New Passage Halt which opened 9 July 1928 and closed 23 November 1964. Cross Hands Halt was similar to New Passage Halt and had identical opening and closing dates, as did Pilning Low Level, approximately sited on the earlier Pilning station on the New Passage Pier

A Dean Goods 0-6-0 has arrived at Severn Beach with a 10-coach train numbered 276.
Author's collection

The spacious concourse at Severn Beach. Author's collection

Single line tablet exchange at Severn Beach signal box 3 June 1963. Author

Pump house siding and pump house for the Severn Tunnel. The pumping beam protrudes from the building. Author's collection

The closed agent's booking office at New Passage Halt circa 1955. Dr A.J.G. Dickens

4-6-0 No 5919 *Worsley Hall* hauls a banana train through New Passage Halt 28 September 1959. Author's collection

Cross Hands Halt and Pilning fixed distant signal circa 1962. The bridge allowed for track doubling. Lens of Sutton

Pilning Low Level Halt circa 1962. The main line is on the right at a higher level. Notice the 9½ mile post (from Temple Meads) by the waiting shelter. Lens of Sutton

line. Beyond the line rose to the main line on the east side of Pilning High Level station.

The Severn Tunnel

Work on the 4½ mile long tunnel, one of the greatest engineering features of the British Isles, began on 18 March 1873 and was fraught with difficulties and dangers. In October 1879 the workings under the land became flooded by the Great Spring. This was very surprising, as everyone had supposed that the tunnel's chief danger was from an influx of river water and none believed that hidden under the land lay a greater difficulty and danger than any to be met with under the bed of the river.

Numerous pumps were installed to drain the various workings, but problems were far from being over as in July 1880 a large pump broke and left water to fill the main shaft. In their haste to escape from this heading, men left open an iron door a thousand feet from the foot of the shaft. As one diver was unable to drag that length of hose, a team of three was used: one stayed at the foot of the shaft; another went forward 500ft and fed hose to a third diver, called Lambert, who groped in total darkness among tools, rock and other debris and, when only 100ft from the door, was too exhausted to pull the hose any further so had to return.

A new patent diving dress invented by Fleuss, with an oxygen pack replacing the air hose, was put to the test three times by Fleuss himself, but was unsuccessful. Lambert donned it and succeeded in reaching the door, pulled up one obstructing rail and then had to return. Two days later he made another trip, pulled up the second rail, closed the door, screwed the valve round the a number of times he had been told it would take to shut it, but still the pumps experienced difficulty in lowering the water level. Two months later the pumps succeeded in draining the heading and it was found that the valve had a left-handed screw and instead of closing it, Lambert had inadvertently turned it fully open!

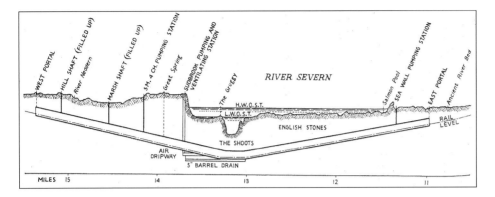

The next problem was the Great Blizzard of 1881 which blocked the railway lines and prevented coal from being delivered to the steam pumps. When coal supplies became exhausted, timber was used as fuel and the pumps were kept going until coal was restored.

On another occasion water burst through the roof of the tunnel near the eastern bank from a part of the river known as 'The Salmon Pool'. It being only about 3ft deep at low tide, the hole was located by men walking through the pool holding hands until one fell out of sight. He was quickly pulled out by his colleagues and the hole plugged with clay.

Modern methods were used by the contractor. Illumination was by electric light and rock was drilled by compressed air tools, while steam navvies were used to excavate the deep cutting on the Gloucestershire side.

In 1882 a telephone connected the works both sides of the river. The first day it was working, it prevented a strike. Just as the principal foreman went into one telephone cabin, he heard a well-known voice at the other end swearing, grumbling and saying that he would advise the men what to do if a grievance was not corrected. The speaker little thought that all he was saying was being overheard by his boss in the other cabin and his instant dismissal prevented him calling a strike.

1883 proved a particularly bad year. On 9 February a workman at the top of a shaft, thinking that the cage on one side was at ground level when it was not, pushed an iron skip down. It fell to the bottom, killing three men in the cage standing at the foot of the shaft and then rebounded into a crowd, killing one and injuring two more.

On 10 October 1883, the night shift was just entering the heading about 6.00pm and had just reached the face and were clearing away the material blown down by the day shift, when in the words of the ganger, 'The water broke in from the bottom of the face, rolling up at once like a great horse' and swept men and skips out of the heading back into the finished tunnel. The Great Spring had been tapped again and once more Lambert had to be sent for to close the door.

No tide had ever been known to come as high as the mouths of the shafts, but on 17 October 1883, when one of the highest tides of the year was due, a south westerly storm was blowing. A wave five to six feet high swept through the workmen's houses, extinguished the fires in the pump and winding house and fell 100ft down the shaft. The men below ran to the cage to be hoisted up, but could not be raised as the water had extinguished the boiler fires of the lift.

Four men climbed an upright ladder against the shaft wall, one man being washed off and killed. Most of the men retreated to the higher workings. Water rose in this tunnel to within 8ft of the crown of the arch, imprisoning 83 men. The contractors obtained a small boat, lowered it end-on down the shaft, but found difficulty in floating it. Eventually they made it dive and then baled it out. After sawing through the timber staging, the men were rescued on the morning following the flooding.

Tidal water filled cuttings at both ends of the tunnels, but as the headings were not yet joined to the cuttings, none of this water got into the tunnel below the river. The mouths of the tunnel were surrounded by 16ft high banks and it was just as well that they were, for about 1910 the sea came in and isolated Severn Beach for three weeks. The embankments were built several feet above the level of the highest recorded tide. These banks cost nothing, for the saving in the cost of tipping the excavated earth there, rather than moving it further, more than paid for the cost of the additional land required.

On 27 October 1884, Sir Daniel Gooch, chairman of the GWR and the Earl of Bessborough, a director, were just able to pass through the tunnel from the cutting on the Gloucestershire side to the cutting on the Monmouthshire shore. On 5 September the following year, Sir Daniel was able to pass through the tunnel by train. Later it was found that the pressure

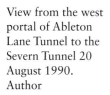

View from the west portal of Ableton Lane Tunnel to the Severn Tunnel 20 August 1990. Author

of the Great Spring was breaking bricks and that instead of trying to contain the Spring, a new shaft would have to be dug to continually pump it. Water gushed out at an average of 24 million gallons a day, which in 1886 was enough to have supplied Liverpool or Manchester. The boring of the tunnel made most of the neighbouring wells go dry, so the railway had to make good this loss by piping water to surrounding villages.

On 1 September 1886 the tunnel was open to goods traffic. On 17 November the Board of Trade inspector passed the tunnel for passenger traffic, a local service commencing on 1 December 1886 nearly 14 years after the works were first started. Seventy five minutes were saved on a journey between Newport and Bristol. The first passenger train from London to South Wales passed through the tunnel on 1 July 1887. The estimated cost of the tunnel had been £900,000, but the actual cost over twice this sum. For many years it remained the world's longest underwater tunnel.

Safety was, and is, of vital importance in the tunnel. In the days of loose coupled freight and mineral wagons, there was always the danger of coupling chains breaking. This was because the tunnel had a V-section longitudinally. Going downhill wagons ran forwards, the buffers touched and the chains were slack. Then, as the train started climbing, the weight of the wagons pulled the couplings tight and if this happened suddenly, a weak link could break, dividing the train. To keep as many coupling chains as taut as possible a guard was required to screw his brake on hard and keep it applied until his van passed to the ascending gradient. Drivers and guards were warned of the change of gradient in the centre of the tunnel by one white light being fixed a quarter of a mile, and two lights at 40yd, from where the falling gradient became level.

In the event of danger, those on the outside of the tunnel could be alerted by the severing of a wire on the tunnel wall which caused an electric bell to ring in signal boxes at both ends of the tunnel. Additionally, 17 illuminated emergency telephones situated in the tunnel recesses gave direct communication.

During WW2 the tunnel caused a bottleneck, every coal train through displacing three faster-moving passenger trains, the average time taken to pass the 4½ mile tunnel section being: passenger 7 minutes; goods 20 minutes. Wartime needs overrode peacetime safety precautions. The long block section between the East and West signal boxes at either end of the tunnel needed breaking up, but previously the Ministry of Transport would not allow intermediate colour light signals for fear of steam in the tunnel obscuring their visibility. In November 1941 special high-intensity lights were installed.

The section could not be exactly halved because if trains stopped at the foot of the incline, they would have experienced difficulty in starting. Therefore the signals were placed approximately two-thirds of the way down the slope so that locomotives could get speed up before encountering the rising gradient. To guard against an adverse signal not being sighted in the smoke, repeater signals were situated nearer the entrance. Additionally there was an Automatic Train Control (ATC) ramp to give drivers an audio and visual indication of the signal, this being actually in the locomotive cab.

Engines not fitted with this ATC apparatus were required to stop and advise the signalman who had then to ensure that the line through the tunnel was clear of traffic before allowing that train to proceed. These electric signals approximately doubled the capacity of the tunnel. The lights were found to be unsatisfactory for peacetime requirements and were removed in 1948.

As a safety precaution, gun powder vans, either loaded or empty, were banned from the tunnel, as were gas tank vehicles. In case of emergency, fire brigades could use a special train including four ex-milk tank wagons filled with water, other wagons carrying pumps and a van containing breathing apparatus. One emergency train was stabled at Pilning and the other at Severn Tunnel Junction. One vehicle was a standard GWR brake van modified to have end-opening doors at the verandah to allow a stretcher or other article to be moved in or out. It was supplied with first aid equipment and had large lights at the front. It was propelled through the tunnel by a banker. If a body was found, the train reversed and collected an ambulance placed on a car-carrying train.

For a period each year, absolute occupation of both tracks is granted from 6.00am until 5.00pm, local traffic formerly being diverted over the Severn Bridge, and mainline traffic via Gloucester. Each square yard of brickwork is struck with a hammer, any areas that sound hollow, or in which scaling has developed, being noted for repair. Two inspection trains move forward side by side, the roof being reached by men standing on the roofs of special tunnel inspection vans and using long-handled hammers.

Heavy trains had an assistant engine coupled in front of the train engine to help on the tunnel gradients. Human nature being what it is, sometimes the crew of the train engine let the banking engine do most of the work. In such an event, the ploy was for the fireman on the first engine to throw rotten fish heads into his firebox to create such a stench that the crew of the second engine were only too glad to make their engine work hard in order to reach fresh air as soon as possible.

In the Severn Tunnel a Matisa ballast cleaner discharges spoil into a wagon. Author's collection

9 GWR Main Line: Chipping Campden to Adlestrop

THE LINE between Campden and Adlestrop was part of the Oxford, Worcester & Wolverhampton Railway, (OWWR), known from its initials as the 'Old Worse & Worse' It obtained its Act on 4 August 1845 to construct a broad gauge line, and like the GWR, employed Brunel as engineer.

By the beginning of 1847 2,800 men were at work building the 90 miles of line, but in the autumn, a financial crisis caused the failure of banks and little cash was available for railway building. Trouble was compounded by a misunderstanding with the GWR which had undertaken to work the line. As relationships between the two companies grew more frigid, Brunel's tenure as engineer to both became impossible, so he resigned his post on the OWWR in March 1852, several months before the major sections of the line were completed. His office was filled by John Fowler, a man later to become famous for his joint design, with Benjamin Baker, of the Forth Bridge, which, at the that time, was the greatest railway bridge in the world.

The most important engineering feature on the OWWR is the 887yd long Campden (or Mickleton) Tunnel. Work was begun in the summer of 1846 and following a change of contractor, R.M. Marchant, one of Brunel's young assistant engineers and also a relative, sought permission to leave Brunel's employ and go into partnership with the new contractor. This Brunel gave, though warning him that it could be financially disastrous. Then in 1849 just as the preliminary headings had been driven through and shafts sunk to open up extra faces and work on the brick lining had begun at both ends, action had to be suspended due to the financial crisis which caused the OWWR to owe Marchant £4,300.

In June 1851, not long after the resumption of work which included laying mixed gauge, Marchant had a dispute with the OWWR over compensation for the suspension of works and things again came to a standstill. It ended in Brunel dismissing Marchant in July. The OWWR not wishing to have the line's opening delayed, took possession of the works and contractor's plant and handed them to Messrs Peto & Betts who were completing the rest of the line.

On Friday 18 July 1851, Brunel and his resident assistant, R. Varden, arrived at Campden Tunnel with 300 men to take possession. Marchant, warned that they were coming, armed his 100 men with clubs and saw that James Ashwin, a County Magistrate was in attendance, the latter warning Brunel not to fight. Brunel hoped his opponents would think that he had been fobbed off and postponed action until the following day, but found 'the magistrates were early on the ground, attended by a large body of police armed with cutlasses. Mr Brunel was there with his men, and Mr Marchant, the Contractor, also appeared at the head of a formidable body of navigators. A conflict was expected, but happily through the prompt action of the magistrates, who twice read the Riot Act to the men, they were dispersed.'

Brunel could not be defeated so easily. On Sunday evening men employed by Peto & Betts began to assemble and by midnight, seven or eight contingents of roughly 250 navvies were converging towards the tunnel on foot and by wagon. At 5.00am on Monday, Marchant's men were confronted with Brunel's army of 2,000. Captain Lefroy and his 30 policemen from Cheltenham stood by, only once interfering when they pounced on one of Peto & Betts' men who was carrying pistols. Brunel's solicitor, Mr Hobler, was in attendance and he and James Ashman, the County Magistrate who was determined to prevent forcible seizure, engaged in 'warm legal discussion'. Eventually Brunel and Marchant signed a document agreeing to put the dispute regarding compensation to arbitration, Brunel promising to give work to William & Marchant's navvies, and to order Peto & Betts to leave the site if arbitration went against the OWWR. Matters now being amicably settled, Captain Lefroy sent a messenger to halt a contingent of troops on their way from Coventry. Although the dramatic account in *The Times* records great violence, in actual fact the scene was relatively peaceful, all being calm by 8.30am, the men recommencing work in the tunnel that morning. The tunnel was finally completed in 1852.

That was not the only conflict in which the tunnel appeared. A temporary village had been set up for tunnel workers and in the summer of 1847, the shopkeepers of Chippping Campden complained to the OWWR directors that because of the 'truck' system, they had been robbed 'of the opportunity to engage in fair and open trading' and were left 'to bear all the loss and inconvenience occasioned by the influx of so many unworthy characters' into their district. The truck system was payment in goods or tickets, instead of cash. The tickets could be exchanged for goods, but were only valid at a shop connected with the railway contractor, some unscrupulous ones, having a captive market, sold poor goods at high prices, giving short weight. Some railway contractors made more money from truck than from the railway contract.

The first contractors at Mickleton operated the system, defying a clause in their contract which prevented it, claiming that the Chipping Campden shopkeepers had formed a cartel to raise prices for the provisions required by the navvies. The truck tickets issued by Warden & Gale and their successors Williams & Ackroyd, could only be exchanged at one shop in Campden and its owner gave the contractors a discount of five to ten per cent on all goods purchased. Lord Sandon of Norton Hall supported the other tradesmen against the contractors and the unfair practice ceased.

Staff were appointed to the new line in April 1853, clerks being paid about £60 annually, the figure varying according to the importance of the station. A porter's weekly wage of 16 shillings compared very favourably with an agricultural worker's nine shillings.

A party of directors travelled over the line on 2 April and it was anticipated that the ceremonial opening would be on 21 April 1853, but the weather had not been reckoned with and rain caused a series of earth slips. The worst occurred in the cutting immediately north of Campden Tunnel where the ballast began to rise. The permanent way was packed with heavy longitudinal timbers, but continued to go up. Still more packing was put below the track until, to quote David Joy, the company's locomotive superintendent, it was 'nearly twice the height of a man over the other road'. The appearance of this packing led to the tunnel being known familiarly as the 'Birdcage'.

The ceremonial opening eventually took place on 7 May 1853, the returning inaugural train of 26 coaches drawn by two locomotives unfortunately killing the watchman stationed at the Birdcage. The single line was

A 0-6-0ST heads an Up train at Moreton in Marsh circa 1905. Beyond the water crane, right, is a gentlemen's cast iron urinal. Author's collection

G.W.R. Station, Moreton.

opened to the public on 4 June 1853, the OWWR using some of its own standard gauge rolling stock and hiring the remainder from the London & North Western Railway. Because of the company's poverty-stricken condition, its locomotives were in a poor state, so much so that on 18 October 1855 the Down evening express was no less than six hours late caused by the successive failure of four locomotives. On 1 July 1860 the OWWR became part of the West Midland Railway which in turn was absorbed by the GWR on 1 August 1863.

This company developed the line which had been doubled between 1853-8. In January 1966 some of the stations and halts closed and much of it was singled in 1971 to effect further economies. Because of the restricted line capacity due to this singling, regular freight traffic ceased.

The most famous station on the line was Adlestrop, immortalised by Edward Thomas's poem. Although the station no longer exists, a GWR seat, the name board and a copy of the poem are preserved in the village bus shelter.

Blockley, view Down circa 1905. Author's collection

A Paddington to Worcester express passes Adlestrop circa 1910. Author's collection

Adlestrop, view Down 1933. Author's collection

10 GWR Main Line: Cheltenham to Toddington

ON 1 AUGUST 1899 the Cheltenham & Honeybourne Railway Act received Royal Assent. This railway, together with existing lines, offered the GWR a new route between Birmingham, Gloucester, Bristol and the South west.

The contractors Messrs Walter Scott & Middleton started work at Honeybourne towards the end of 1902, and was opened in sections, the line

Advertisement for an excursion to visit the Great Exhibition, *Gloucester Journal* 7 June 1851.

Widening Lansdown Junction, Cheltenham 1942: LMS left, GWR right. Today there are just two tracks. The signal box still stands, but is bricked up. Photo: GWR

Cheltenham Malvern Road 11 April 1940, LNER J25 class 0-6-0 No 2076. It was on loan to the GWR from November 1939 until November 1946. Local railwaymen referred to the class as 'Teddy Bears' as their cabs were more comfortable to work in than Dean Goods. Leslie Lapper

4-6-0 No 7815
Fritwell Manor at
Cheltenham
Malvern Road shed
2 October 1949.
W. Potter

reaching Toddington 1 December 1904, Winchcombe 1 February 1905, Bishop's Cleeve 1 June 1906 and Cheltenham 1 August 1906.

The new line was used mainly by local traffic, passenger trains using the existing St James' station at Cheltenham until the Stratford on Avon branch had been doubled, but when this task was completed late in 1907, through goods traffic began, followed in the summer of 1908 by passenger trains. It was the introduction of these through trains which caused Malvern Road station to be built. Cheltenham being an important stop on the Birmingham to Bristol route, GWR trains would have had to reverse into St James'– a time-consuming operation. To obviate this need, a station was built at Malvern Road on the through line. As a WW1 economy measure, Malvern Road was closed from 1 January 1917 until 7 July 1919. On 1 February 1925 'Spa' was added to the name.

Stanway Viaduct
north of
Toddington
showing the arches
which have
collapsed. Of the
ten completed
arches, three fell on
13 November 1903
and another the
following day. This
resulted in the
deaths of four men,
plus injury to
several others.
Note the
contractor's
impermanent way
beside the piers.
Author's collection

The first steam rail motor approaches Cheltenham St James' station at 8.51am 1 August 1906. Author's collection

Cheltenham St James' station 6 May 1960. Author

The carriage approach to Cheltenham Spa (St James') station circa 1963. Lens of Sutton

Gloucestershire Engineering Society's excursion from Cheltenham to Winchcombe 19 May 1906 along the unfinished line. The locomotive is the contractor Walter Scott & Middleton's *Pallion*, Manning Wardle 0-6-0ST works No 1525. Author's collection

Alstone Avenue built by the GWR to house people displaced by building the line to Honeybourne. Author

The Cheltenham, St James to Honeybourne local passenger service was withdrawn from 7 March 1960. From 10 September 1962 'The Cornishman' and the South Wales diesel multiple unit trains were diverted via Ashchurch, but summer-only trains continued to use the Honeybourne route on Friday nights and Saturdays until 1966. On 3 January 1966 Malvern Road and St James' stations both closed and the Cheltenham to Toddington line itself shut 25 August 1976. Fortunately it was not the end of the story and the Gloucestershire Warwickshire Railway has succeeded in reopening the Gloucestershire section of the line.

Leaving Malvern Road the line passed High Street Halt opened 1 October 1908 and closed 30 April 1917. Beyond the 97yd long Hunting Butts Tunnel, Cheltenham Racecourse station opened 13 March 1912. It was cunningly provided with strong barriers to guard against the crush and only permitted passengers to emerge in three streams, thus making life difficult for fare evaders. Bishop's Cleeve and Gotherington stations were of typical GWR contemporary design, but in stone rather than brick. Gretton Halt opened 1 June 1906 and was unusual in that it was inaugurated with the line, rather than being an afterthought like most halts. One of its more famous users was L. T. C. Rolt, the transport author. Greet Tunnel is 695yd in length. Following the line's closure, Winchcombe was demolished, but the Gloucestershire Warwickshire Railway has transferred the building from Monmouth Troy, while a replacement signal box came from Hall Green. Hayles Abbey Halt, opened 24 September 1928 and Toddington was the last station on the line in Gloucestershire. Although the village of Weston sub Edge was in Gloucestershire, its station was in Worcestershire.

A 28XX class 2-8-0 leaving Hunting Butts Tunnel with a Down goods July 1941. W. Potter

Cheltenham Racecourse station from the north 19 April 1968. Author

The Winchcombe to Cheltenham auto train hauled by 517 class 0-4-2T No 562 near Cheltenham Racecourse 24 July 1924. H.G.W. Household

Engineer's inspection saloon at Gotherington 26 July 1906. Author's collection

4-6-0 No 7024 *Powis Castle* passes Bishop's Cleeve 27 July 1963 with a Wolverhampton to Paignton express. W. Potter

Hayles Abbey Halt, view Up. P. J. Garland

Toddington, view
Up. A large water
tank is set on the
embankment.
P.J.Garland

Fruit baskets at
Toddington circa
1905. Author's
collection

Weston sub Edge,
an early view with
a steam rail motor
to Cheltenham.
Author's collection

11 GWR Branch Line: Cheltenham to Stow on the Wold

THIS WAS another line linking the Midlands with the South West. The first part of it in Gloucestershire was the Bourton on the Water Railway which received an Act 14 June 1860 to build a branch from Kingham, on the OWWR in Oxfordshire, just over the county boundary. The Bourton line opened 1 March 1862 and like so many small companies was worked by a larger, in this case the West Midland Railway.

For a railway to be profitable, it needed to be part of a through route, so extensions were planned to Banbury in the north and Cheltenham in the south. To this end the Banbury & Cheltenham Direct Railway Act was passed 21 July 1873. Active work began in November 1874, but shareholders became somewhat apprehensive when the financial crisis of 1878 caused work to be suspended for over a year. Cheltenham to Bourton was opened 1 June 1881 and on 1 July 1897 the line was purchased by the GWR for £138,000. Between May 1906 and September 1939 the line was used by the Ports to Ports Express, linking Newcastle upon Tyne with Gloucester, Newport, Cardiff, Barry and Swansea. Another interesting train was the Great Central Railway's special day excursion to Fishguard for Killarney.

An interesting, but little known fact is that during WW2, in the event of a breakdown of telecommunication between major GWR centres, the Postmaster General issued transmitting and receiving licences for four fixed station, nine rail and three mobile units. One of the mobile units set up in an old coach with sleeping and cooking facilities was at Charlton Kings, while one of the road units was at Gloucester.

Cheltenham Leckhampton, view north circa 1963. Lens of Sutton

A steam crane working at Old Bath Road Bridge, Leckhampton struck by a bomb 11 December 1940. Author's collection

The very pleasant setting of Charlton Kings, view towards Andoversford 6 May 1960. Author

After WW2 the line fell into decline and heavy mineral traffic decreased. Passenger traffic ceased 15 October 1962 when Cheltenham to Bourton on the Water closed completely. Bourton remained open for goods until 7 September 1964 – a sad end to a route which at one time offered the shortest, quickest and cheapest way from Cheltenham to London.

Passenger trains left Cheltenham St James and curved round to Leckhampton. When it became the Cheltenham station for the Ports to Ports Express, it was renamed Leckhampton & Cheltenham South, altered in 1952 to Cheltenham & Leckhampton. Between 1922-6 a 1¼ mile long mineral branch ran from Charlton Kings to Leckhampton Quarries. Beyond Charlton Kings the main line ran parallel with a reservoir for half a mile to the 192yd long Woodbank Viaduct and the 384yd Andoversford Tunnel. From 1 August

1891 Andoversford was the junction with the Midland & South Western Junction Railway (see page 119) and due to the increase in traffic over the section between Cheltenham and Andoversford, the single line was doubled in 1902.

5101 class 2-6-2T No 4100 at Andoversford with the 1.15pm Kingham to Cheltenham St James' 4 October 1962. Author's collection

Notgrove station, 760ft above sea level, was claimed to be the highest of any GWR through route in England. Bourton on the Water station was originally of half-timbered construction, but in the nineteen-thirties was rebuilt in Cotswold stone with a stone tiled roof, creating a pleasing design. Stow on the Wold had only a single platform, so trains were unable to cross. It was 475ft above sea level and a mile distant from the town which was almost 300ft higher.

Notgrove station, view towards Bourton on the Water circa 1963. Lens of Sutton

The mock-Tudor station at Bourton on the Water circa 1905. Tourist tickets are advertised to Wales and Ireland. Author's collection

5101 class 2-6-2T No 4143 with a train from Kingham, enters Bourton on the Water circa 1960. T.J.Saunders

The original station building at Stow on the Wold circa 1900. The keys are on the inside of the rails. Author's collection

The nineteen-thirties replacement station at Stow on the Wold. T.J.Saunders

12 GWR Branch Line: South Cerney to Andoversford

THE LINE between South Cerney and Andoversford was part of the Swindon & Cheltenham Extension Railway (SCER) which obtained its Act 18 July 1881, being the last part of a link between the Midlands and the growing port of Southampton. Earl Bathurst who owned nearly 10,000 acres near Cirencester and was a supporter of the SCER, observed that it was impossible to travel to Scotland in a day from the GWR station at Cirencester as the connection arrived at Gloucester one minute after the MR express had left.

In 1883 the contractor suggested that the name 'Swindon & Cheltenham' led potential share subscribers to believe that it was a mere local line and proposed that the name could be changed by amalgamating with the Swindon, Marlborough & Andover Railway and adopting a new name for the combined system. This came about by an Act of 23 June 1884 which formed the Midland & South Western Junction Railway (MSWJR).

Meanwhile the line had been completed between Swindon and Cirencester. Goods traffic started on 1 November 1883, but exceptionally wet weather caused an embankment slip which prevented Major Marindin, the Board of Trade inspector, from passing the line. A second inspection was made on 17 December 1883 and as his train reached South Cerney and Cirencester stations, bills were posted that the line would open on the 18th.

By mid-1884 the MSWJR was in serious financial difficulties and despite economies, was in Receivership by the end of the year and work on the extension to Andoversford had to be halted. In 1887 work was restarted and finished in May 1890. Before the Board of Trade inspection, a section of Chedworth Tunnel collapsed. Repairs were protracted and Major Marindin eventually carried out his inspection on 23 and 24 January 1891. The Board of Trade sanctioned opening on 11 March, but then snow blocked the line and not until the 16th could a train carry the directors, secretary and traffic manager, from Andover to Cheltenham and the line be open to two daily freight trains.

It offered an efficient service: goods collected in London in the late afternoon were delivered the next morning in Cirencester and Cheltenham. Through passenger services could not be started until alterations had been made at the MR's Cheltenham Lansdown station. In July 1891 the MR sent a telegram: 'If you can arrange to work your engines without turning at Cheltenham the rest of the work will be ready for opening on the first proximo' [1 August]. This offer was accepted and through traffic began. Traffic developed to such an extent that the Receiver was discharged in 1897. Much of the MSWJR was doubled, but not the Swindon to Cirencester section.

Cirencester. The porter has left his brush and sweepings near the foot of the water tower while the photograph was taken. The channel for signal wires can be seen lower left. Author's collection

The MSWJR proved vital during WW1, not only serving military camps on Salisbury Plain, but carrying war supplies southwards and ambulance trains northwards. Engine drivers were sometimes so busy that they did not see their families for a fortnight. The MSWJR locomotive stud was insufficient to handle all the trains so engines were loaned by the GWR, MR and the London & South Western Railway.

The Railways Act of 1921 allowed the GWR to absorb the MSWJR. With hindsight this was a mistake. The GWR did little to encourage traffic over the route, whereas had it become a joint LMS/SR line like the Somerset & Dorset Railway, traffic would have been developed.

Following a resurgence during WW2 when it again became a vital north to south route, there was a gradual decline and the withdrawal of passenger trains from 9 September 1961 saw the closure of most of the former MSWJR, but diesel-hauled goods trains ran between Swindon and Cirencester until 1 April 1964.

The MSWJR owned quite a respectable stud of locomotives, mostly 0-6-0s and 4-4-0s. In 1895 it bought a 2-6-0 and at the time of purchase

was the only example of that wheel arrangement in the country. It proved a success and a further engine was bought in 1897, the same year as two handsome 4-4-4 tank engines were purchased for use on stopping passenger trains, this wheel arrangement being suited to the many reverse curves. One driver said; 'They rode like a cradle'. Following absorption, the GWR Swindonised many of the MSWJR engines with taper boilers and GWR cabs. The last MSWJR engine to be withdrawn was 2-4-0 No 1336 in 1954.

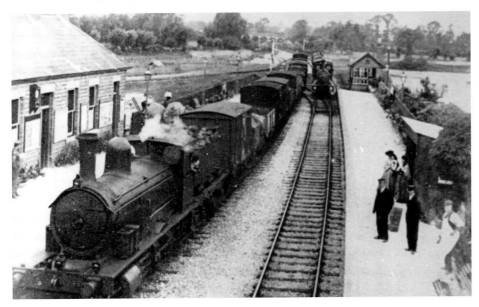

A MSWJR 2-6-0 at South Cerney circa 1905. A Down passenger train, right, is overtaking the goods train, left. Author's collection

August 1914 marked the peak of MSWJR services. Two South Expresses ran to Southampton from Birmingham and Manchester respectively. On Sundays two trains ran each way plus the North Express. Trains consisted of eight to nine coaches. WW1 caused through coaches to be withdrawn, but in 1922 a through coach was introduced running from Liverpool and continued until the outbreak of WW2. In 1955 three trains ran between Cheltenham Lansdown and Andover Junction, but a drastic cut on 30 June 1958 left only one. Track changes at Lansdown Junction robbed MSWJR of its route into Lansdown station, so the surviving train was diverted to Cheltenham St James, thus discouraging its use by any passengers from the North.

The preserved 4-4-0 No 3440 *City of Truro* hauls the Down Gloucestershire Railway Society special at Foss Cross. Author's collection

Chedworth circa 1899 showing the temporary building part of which was a grounded coach body. Stationmaster Freddy Tucker, Porter 'Curly' Beames and Platelayer George Rook are depicted. The track has inside keys; the notice boards belong to the Midland Railway. The sack trucks bear the station name. The building was moved to the other side of the line and then placed on the Down platform. Author's collection

Some goods trains ran quite swiftly: the 3.00am from Cheltenham arrived at Southampton at 7.20am having covered the 90½ miles at an average running speed of 24mph. It was followed by the 4.45am taking only ten minutes longer. The 9.30pm Southampton to Cheltenham made an average speed of over 25mph – excellent considering that much of it was over single track.

In 1927 the line between South Cerney and Cirencester was used for an experiment with the Motor Economic System of permanent way maintenance, permitting three gang-lengths to be worked by only one gang. Telephone and electric token boxes were installed at intervals along the line

Chedworth, view north: the waiting shelter, left, originally came from the first station at Chedworth. Author's collection

Andoversford & Dowdeswell station, view Down circa 1935. The station closed to passengers 1 April 1927 and the building was subsequently used as a café as it fronted the A40. Author's collection

and allowed a mechanically-propelled trolley, carrying personnel and equipment, to be taken off the track in mid-section, the restoration of a key in a lineside box enabling a train token to be released in a signal box. The idea proved a success and was extended over other parts of the GWR.

A permanent way trolley at Cirencester 1929. It has a turntable and rails so that it can be moved off the track when the gangers are working. Top left is the locomotive works closed 26 October 1925. Author's collection

13 GWR Branch Lines: Including Gloucester to Dymock and Grange Court to Hopesbrook

Gloucester to Dymock

THE FIRST alternative to road transport between Gloucester and Ledbury was the Herefordshire & Gloucestershire Canal, opened to Ledbury in 1798, its principal feature being the 2,192yd long Oxenhall Tunnel between Newent and Dymock.

In 1845, the year of the Railway Mania when so many new lines were being projected all over the country, the directors saw the possibilities of jumping on the band wagon and converting their canal into a railway. Their plans met with little success until 1861 when the Ledbury & Gloucester Railway was proposed, backed by the West Midland Railway and included the conversion of Oxenhall Tunnel to railway use. In the event, this interesting scheme proved abortive.

In 1872 two rival schemes were proposed. The first consisted of two separate undertakings under common promotion. One was the Ross & Ledbury Railway running via Dymock and the other the Newent Railway from the GWR near Gloucester, through Newent to join the line from Ross at Dymock. The second scheme, the Ross, Ledbury & Gloucester Railway was very similar, but modified near Gloucester to have its own bridge across the Severn.

Both schemes came before Parliament in 1873, the latter plan being successfully opposed by the Severn Commissioners on the grounds that a separate bridge would have offered insufficient clearance for navigation. The

Ross & Ledbury obtained its Act on 28 July 1873 and the associated Newent Company also being successful eight days later.

Both companies planned to make extensive use of the course of the Herefordshire & Gloucestershire Canal in the construction of their lines. The Newent Railway was empowered to convert the Oxenhall Tunnel to railway use, but the idea was abandoned, a deviation avoiding the high ground between Newent and Dymock being authorised in 1874.

Little progress was achieved until agreement was reached with the GWR in May 1876 to subscribe the necessary capital. The GWR insisted that the existing directors retire in favour of GWR nominees. This new blood decided not to go ahead with the proposed line between Dymock and Ross.

The contract for the construction of a double line between Ledbury and Dymock was let to Appleby & Lawton in October 1880. Notice was given that the canal would be closed to traffic after 30 June 1881, although there is evidence that the southern half was used by the railway contractors for almost nine months after this date. In January 1883 the tender of the same firm of contractors was accepted for building the line from Dymock to the junction with the GWR at Over. Earthworks were to be wide enough for double track, but only a single line was laid.

Colonel Rich inspected the line on 18 July 1885 and it opened on 27 July. As this coincided with the summer show of the Gloucestershire Agricultural Society, the GWR station at Gloucester was gaily decorated for the dual event, one delight being Chinese lanterns suspended outside the refreshment room. Thirty to forty passengers booked to Dymock by the first train.

The Ledbury line shortened the route from Gloucester to the Birmingham area, though still far from taking a bee-line but offered a valuable saving in mileage compared with the circuitous journey via Hereford. Malswick Halt opened 1 February 1938, Four Oaks Halt 16 October 1937, Greenway Halt 1 April 1937 and Ledbury Town Halt 26 November 1928. As an economy measure, during WW1 branch passenger trains ceased running north of Ledbury and double track between Dymock and Ledbury was singled 4 January 1917.

Diesel railcar No 19 at Newent with the 1.25pm Ledbury to Gloucester Central, 16 May 1959. R.E.Toop

Diesel Railcar No 19 at Four Oaks. Passengers are bound for a shopping trip to Ledbury, 4 April 1959. Children wear short trousers and the guard has a smart white shirt. E. Wilmshurst

Diesel railcar No 19 at Dymock with the 1.25pm Ledbury to Gloucester Central 16 May 1959. R.E.Toop

2251 class 0-6-0 No 3203 at Dymock with the 6.24pm Gloucester to Ledbury, the final Down train 11 July 1959. Hugh Ballantyne

2251 class 0-6-0 No 3203 at Greenway Halt with the 6.24pm Gloucester to Ledbury, 11 July 1959. Hugh Ballantyne

Due to the volume of freight traffic, signal boxes between Newent and Dymock remained open continuously on weekdays. The box at Barber's Bridge was closed at night, an unusual procedure allowing goods trains to pass through the station towards Gloucester on the right, instead of the left hand road, with the signals at danger and the signal lamps extinguished. With the opening of the North Warwickshire on 9 December 1907 improving access to the Toddington to Cheltenham line, all but one of the through goods trains via Newent were immediately diverted to run over the new line instead. In June 1936 the line again saw through trains when one Sunday LMS trains from Gloucester to Birmingham were diverted via Ledbury due to engineering work north of Gloucester.

Because of the short turntable at Ledbury, engines on the branch were required to be fitted with a small tender, though from 1940 most services were worked by a GWR diesel railcar. Bus competition and the use of cars, caused traffic to fall, so the last passenger trains ran on 11 July 1959, goods trains being withdrawn at the end of May 1964.

Diesel railcar No 19 at Gloucester Central 16 May 1959 forming the 12.10pm to Ledbury. R.E.Toop

Grange Court to Hopesbrook

The story of the line between Grange Court and Hopesbrook really began back in the eighteen-forties when Brunel, building the CGWUR felt it should be extended to Hereford. The Hereford, Ross & Gloucester Railway Act was passed 5 June 1851 without opposition – most unusual as there was generally at least one contending party – and tenders for construction were sought. The resident engineer was Charles Richardson, better known for his work as chief engineer to the Severn Tunnel.

Track consisted of special rails invented by William Henry Barlow. Theoretically a good idea, these rails, shaped like a flattened letter 'V' with curved sides, had the advantage that they could be laid directly on the ballast without any timber or other support, ballast being pushed inside the hollow rails and outside just below flange depth to prevent movement. Unfortunately in practice it was found that the hollow section tended to spread under load and so the rails had to be replaced by those of conventional pattern. John William Grover discovered that these Barlow rails could be bent into graceful curves and, when bolted back to back, make strong girders. An example of this use can be seen on Clevedon Pier in North West Somerset.

The first five miles from the junction with the SWR at Grange Court to a temporary station Hopesbrook opposite the eastern portal of the 782yd long Lea Tunnel adjacent to the Mitcheldean turnpike road, was opened on 11 July 1853, worked by the GWR. It opened through to Hereford on 1 June 1855. The GWR absorbed the Hereford, Ross & Gloucester Railway in 1862 and decided to convert it to standard gauge. It was closed from 14–20 August 1869 for this work to be carried out.

During this period, passengers were conveyed between Grange Court and Hereford in hired four-horse London buses, this temporary service starting on Monday 16 August providing the curious sight of buses labelled 'Bayswater', 'Oxford Street' and 'Bank' running along Gloucestershire roads. The work of conversion was unusually difficult due to the tunnels and the fact that at least six different types of rail had been laid at various times, necessitating the use of workmen with wide experience and different types of tools.

450 permanent way men were conveyed to Hereford in three special trains on Saturday 14 August 1869 and a train of 40 broad gauge vans provided for the men to sleep in. The vehicles had been whitewashed inside and clean straw and new sacks supplied for the men's bedding. A first class coach was provided for the accommodation of the officers in charge. An observer reported: 'At four o'clock on Sunday morning the sleeping train was in motion, and an engineer had gone ahead setting up a flag-pole at the end of each gang's length of work for the day. The train stopped at each flag-pole,

Blaisdon Halt, view Down circa 1963. Author's collection

43XX class 2-6-0
No 7318 at
Longhope with a
Gloucester to
Hereford train 23
September 1964.
Derrick Payne

and a ganger and gang of 22 men, furnished with a day's provisions, jumped out with all the necessary tools, also a cask of water, "devil", iron crock and fuel. This process was continued throughout the whole length of the line 450 men could be spread over.

Soon a line of smoke was to be seen ascending, and the work of getting breakfast was actively going on. The men brought their own food – a week's supply – and it was arranged that should the work extend beyond that time through bad weather or any unforeseen circumstances, they were to be allowed to stop for a day to get fresh supplies. Cocoa seemed the favourite beverage, the food various – cold bacon, meat or bread and cheese.

The narrowing was commenced by a gang immediately on its disembarkation, and in about four hours had been completed sufficiently to permit the passing of a narrow [standard] gauge engine very slowly and cautiously driven, over the newly-placed rails. By evening the length was completely finished, packed with ballast, and in good running order. Then commenced the operation of loading up the men and tools into a narrow gauge train, which carried them forward to the end of the length where the broad gauge trains of vans was awaiting them. Next followed a little miscellaneous cooking, a well-earned supper and an early turn-in amongst the straw in the vans preparatory to another day's work commencing at four o'clock next morning.'

Their work consisted of withdrawing 3,800 bolts each mile, or 85,600 in all; drilling the same number of holes in the sleepers and re-fixing the bolts, screwing up the nuts and lifting the rails 27½ inches sideways.

During the Great Blizzard of 1881 three trains and five engines were snowed up between Mitcheldean and Blaisdon. An unusual event took place in October 1886 when a child was born in a railway carriage between Longhope and Grange Court stations.

A through coach from Hereford travelled as a stopping train to Gloucester where it was attached to the Cheltenham Flyer, which in the mid-thirties was the world's fastest train, regularly reaching 80-85mph on its run to London.

Grange Court to Ross, normally a secondary line, was often used as a diversionary route by West to North expresses on winter Sundays when the Severn Tunnel was closed for maintenance.

With the development of road transport in the years following WW2, the line became uneconomic and passenger traffic was withdrawn by Dr Beeching on 2 November 1964, the line being closed completely 1 November 1965.

A Grange Court to Longhope single line tablet. Derrick Payne

A railmotor ticket from the Newnham to Drybrook Halt service.

Bullo Pill Junction to Cinderford and Mitcheldean Road

There were many branch lines and mineral tramways in the Forest of Dean and to avoid this book being dominated by the area, only the principal branches are described, H. W. Parr, I. Pope, B. Howe and P. Karau having written definitive histories listed in Suggested Further Reading.

As there was no passenger station at Bullo Pill Junction, passenger trains for the Cinderford and Mitcheldean Road branch actually commenced at Newnham on the SWR. From Bullo Pill Junction to Cinderford Junction the branch approximately followed the formation of a horse-worked plateway which had a gauge of 3ft 10½ inches and was built under the Bullo Railway Act of 10 June 1809. The Bullo Railway had been purchased by the SWR in 1847 and the SWR New Works Act of 3 July 1851 authorised its reconstruction. It was opened to locomotives 24 July 1854. The Mitcheldean Road & Forest of Dean Junction Railway Act of 13 July 1871, authorised an extension from Cinderford Junction to Mitcheldean Road on the Grange Court to Hereford line.

As the horse-worked line was busy, conversion to broad gauge had to be carried out without interrupting traffic. This was relatively easy in the open air, but widening narrow tunnels with trains continuing to run through, was more difficult. It was only when the tram plates were replaced with rails that the trains were actually halted. The line was duly converted to standard gauge 11-12 May 1872.

The line was not used by passenger trains until the steam rail motor service began between Newnham and Steam Mills Crossing Halt 3 August 1907. This service was extended to Drybrook Halt 4 November 1907 and it was highly unusual for a halt, rather than a station, to be a terminus. Another curiosity was Ruspidge Halt, which had a substantial platform and booking office, rather than a mere shelter with tickets purchased on the train. The passenger service between Cinderford and Drybrook Halt was withdrawn from 7 July 1930 and Cinderford to Bullo Pill 3 November 1958. Freight officially ended 1 August 1967, though the last train actually ran on 2 August 1967.

8750 class 0-6-0PT No 3740 at Staple Edge Halt with the 4.08pm Cinderford to Gloucester Central 25 October 1958. Michael Jenkins

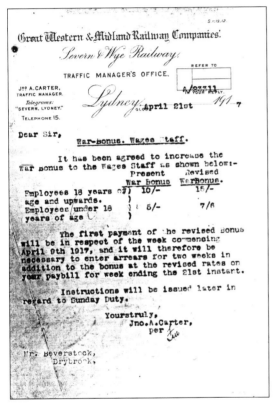

Letter to Mr Beverstock, Drybrook station, in favour of his war bonus.

An auto train at Ruspidge Halt circa 1950. Author's collection

8750 class 0-6-0PT No 3740 at Cinderford with the 2.27pm from Gloucester Central 25 October 1958, comprising two corridor coaches. Michael Jenkins

Cinderford from the buffer stops circa 1908. 2021 class 0-6-0ST and a three coach train is arriving, while another engine of the same class with an auto trailer, is behind the goods shed. Author's collection

Steam rail motor
and trailer No 20
at Steam Mills on 4
November 1907,
the first day that
the service was
extended to
Drybrook.
Author's collection

A two-car auto
train (Car No 42 &
No 43) in all-
brown livery at
Drybrook Halt
circa 1910. Note
the garden in the
foreground.
Author's collection

2021 class 0-6-0ST
No 2118 at
Drybrook Halt circa
1909. Author's
collection

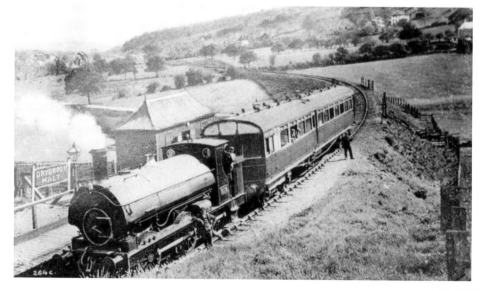

Between Bullo Tunnel, 1,064yd and Bradley Hill Tunnel 299yd, was the
Great Western Iron Company's Soudley furnaces. Blue Rock Tunnel 109yd,
followed, beyond which was Shakemantle Iron Mine. Beyond Drybrook Halt
was the 90yd Drybrook Tunnel and the 634yd Hawthorns Tunnel. Although
track was laid through the tunnel to Mitcheldean Road station, this section
was never opened and was lifted in February 1917.

Lydney to Lydbrook, Coleford and Cinderford

Lydney Town circa 1960. M. Wathen

The Lydney to Lydbrook Junction line began as a horse-worked plateway, authorised by the Lydney & Lidbrook (sic) Railway Act of 10 June 1809. The Severn & Wye Railway Act of 21 June 1810 permitted a name change to the Severn & Wye Railway & Canal. In 1868 from Speech House southwards, a broad gauge line was laid beside the tram road, only to be converted to standard gauge three years later.

The Coleford branch was authorised 18 July 1872 and opened 9 December 1875. In 1879 the Severn & Wye Railway was taken over and worked by the GWR and MR jointly (see page 41) and at one time through passenger trains ran from Berkeley Road over the Severn Bridge to Lydbrook Junction, but from 8 July 1929 were terminated at Lydney Town and no passenger services ran northwards. An interesting feature of the joint line was that unlike the GWR, LMS, LNER and SR, it retained red, as distinct from yellow, distant signals until 1945.

Empty wagons for lifted sleepers, being propelled into Miery Stock Tunnel. Author's collection

Whitecroft circa 1950. Author's collection

Parkend circa 1910. Between the fences in the foreground is the siding to Parkend Goods Depot. Author's collection

Speech House Road
November 1961;
the wood
distillation plant
siding is on the far
left. Michael
Jenkins

Lydbrook Viaduct
11 April 1956.
Author's collection

14XX class 0-4-2T
No 1445 at
Lydbrook Junction
2 June 1951. Peter
Davey

Drybrook Road view west 11 August 1953. This station was closed to passengers 8 July 1929. Dr A.J.G. Dickens

Coleford (Severn & Wye) station circa 1905. Some of the track is flat-bottomed. Author's collection

Newland station
view north circa
1953. It closed to
passengers 1
January 1917.
Author's collection

Newland station view north circa 1953. It closed to passengers 1 January 1917. Author's collection

Lydbrook to Mierystock closed 30 January 1956; the line was cut back to Speech House Road 21 November 1960, though a rail tour reached there on 15 March 1980 and until July 1981 it was used monthly to preserve a right of way. The whole branch was curvaceous and its main engineering features the 242yd Mierystock Tunnel and the 187yd long Lydbrook viaduct. Lydney harbour was important for shipping Forest coal, but dwindling trade caused the branch serving it to be closed 1 September 1963. The Dean Forest Railway set up its base on the site of Norchard colliery and runs trains to Lydbrook Junction and Parkend.

Chepstow to Tintern

The Wye Valley Railway received an Act of Parliament 10 August 1866 to build a line from Chepstow to Monmouth. The southern half of the line was in Gloucestershire, but immediately south of Tintern it crossed the Wye into Monmouthshire.

The contractor began work in May 1874, the 1,190yd long Tidenham Tunnel being the most difficult feature and even boring 24 hours a day with the best equipment available, progress was only two yards a day, so the tunnel took almost two years to complete. North of the tunnel the line emerged on Shorn Cliff, the railway being placed dramatically on a ledge 150ft above the river, making it one of the most scenic lines in the county. Other important engineering features were the 47yd long Black Morgan Viaduct, the 185yd long Tintern Tunnel and the 69yd long Tintern River Bridge across into Monmouthshire. Until about 1935, a branch

The southern portal of Tidenham Tunnel, October 1876. Author's collection

Redbrook, October 1876. Author's collection

nearly ¾ mile in length left the Wye Valley Railway by the southern portal of Tintern Tunnel and crossed the Wye to serve Tintern Abbey Wire Works. This branch has become a public footpath.

The Wye Valley Railway opened 1 November 1876. Worked by the GWR it was eventually taken over by that company in 1905. Passenger services ended 3 January 1959 and goods 6 January 1964, though the southern end of the line remained open for stone traffic from Tintern Quarry until 29 March 1990.

The final passenger train calls at Redbrook 4 January 1959. It is hauled by 64XX class 0-6-0PT No 6439 and is a Stephenson Locomotive Society special. Author's collection

37275 hauls
wagons under the
loading gantry at
Dayhouse Quarry.
The platform, right,
was Tidenham
Halt. Paul Strong

Unusually, passenger trains did not start at Wye Valley Junction where the branch left the main line, nor at Chepstow, the nearest important station, but at Portskewett Pier, served by a ferry across the Severn from New Passage. With the opening of the Severn Tunnel, the pier became redundant, so from 1 December 1886, Severn Tunnel Junction became the terminus. From 1932 the auto trains were based at Newport and from June 1939 some services were operated by a diesel railcar. The only stations on the branch in Gloucestershire were Tidenham and Netherhope Halt, the latter opening 16 May 1932.

Wye Valley
Junction: 2301
class 0-6-0 carrying
express headlights
works a Down
train 'wrong road',
September 1945.
Peter Davey

Fairford station set in rural surroundings. Author's collection

Fairford to Lechlade

The line between Fairford and Lechlade was built by the East Gloucestershire Railway which received an Act 7 August 1862 to build a line between Witney and Fairford. Shortage of funds delayed construction and it was not opened until 15 January 1873 and was taken over by the working company, the GWR, 1 July 1890. As through routes, rather than terminal branches, were lines that paid good dividends, it was always hoped that it would be extended from Fairford to Cheltenham or Cirencester. Certainly Fairford station had the appearance of a through station.

8750 class 0-6-0PT No 4676 waiting by Fairford goods shed circa 1960 before returning to Oxford. Author's collection

As early as 1897 a solid tyred, oil burning, steam driven motor van carrying three tons of parcels and drawing a 20-seater passenger trailer, linked the MSWJR station at Cirencester with Fairford and between 29 October 1928 and 7 February 1932, the GWR operated a bus service between Cheltenham and Oxford. The branch closed to both goods and passenger traffic 10 August 1962.

In 1906 the branch was the first single line on the GWR to be equipped for Automatic Train Control (ATC) working, an ingenious system whereby a driver was given an audible warning if he passed a signal at danger. Previous experiments had been on double track and the system required modification for use on a single line. So successful was it that every distant signal between Yarnton Junction, near Oxford, and Fairford was abolished and replaced by an ATC ramp.

The Cirencester to Fairford road train at Cirencester 1897. The Liquid Fuel Engineering Company's 35hp van/tractor is hauling a 20-seater trailer. Author's collection

14 GWR Branch Lines: Kemble to Tetbury, Kemble to Cirencester

Kemble to Tetbury

O N 28 AUGUST 1872 Colonel Nigel Kingscote MP called a public meeting 'To consider the propriety of taking the necessary steps for obtaining railway communication between the Town of Tetbury and the Great Western Railway near Kemble Junction'. Although Miss Anna Gordon agreed to a railway crossing her estate from a junction with the GWR at Tetbury Road station, she found the idea of a junction at Kemble (hitherto merely a platform for changing trains and with no public access) unacceptable. Agreeing with her would have meant that the junctions of the Cirencester and Tetbury branches would have been a mile apart and as this would have been unacceptable to the GWR; negotiations continued, with the result that Kemble was made a public station.

The GWR's Tetbury branch was authorised by the GWR (No 1) Act, 7 August 1884 and relatively unusual in that it was a branch line built by a large company rather than a local concern. J. Harris of Brighton was given the contract to build the line and the first sod was turned at Kemble 18 October 1887. No important constructional features were required and the line opened just over two years later on 2 December 1889. Traffic on the line received a boost when, four years later, a cattle market opened at Tetbury.

Jackaments Bridge Halt opened 3

Rodmarton Platform 30 March 1956. Author

July 1939 for the benefit of RAF personnel at Kemble airfield. Rodmarton Platform opened 1 September 1904, had the honour of being the first GWR 'platform', the term borrowed by the company from Scotland where the word was used to distinguish it from a 'halt'. A halt was generally unstaffed, but a platform was staffed by a senior grade porter who booked passengers, parcels and milk traffic.

The original station at Tetbury was built of timber so that in the event of the line being extended, it could easily be moved. In 1916 it was reconstructed in brick, many of the windows and doors being recycled. An interesting feature of the station drive was that, before boundary revision, it was divided between Gloucestershire and Wiltshire.

The original timber-built Tetbury station, 1914. Note the canopy supports. Author's collection

Tetbury station circa 1905. Author's collection

'Mixed' trains, that is combined passenger and goods trains, were worked by a small tank engine kept overnight in the shed at Tetbury. A nearby well supplied all the locomotive's water needs, this being raised by a steam pump which received its supply from the engine.

The branch featured in two experiments. In 1926 the GWR purchased two patent geared, four-wheeled steam locomotives from the Sentinel Wagon Works. They had a vertical, rather than horizontal boilers and set within the cab, rather than at one end. Capable of a speed of 18mph, No 12 was tested on the Tetbury branch, but was not a success.

Real economy was effected 33 years later when railbuses were introduced on 2 February 1959. The number of services on the branch was increased

A group, mainly railway staff, around 517 class 0-4-2T No 520 at Tetbury. This locomotive was withdrawn in October 1912. Author's collection

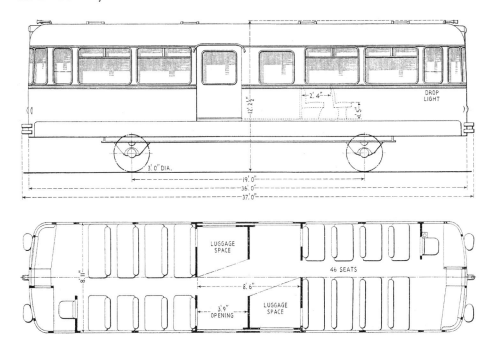

AC Cars 150hp rail bus.

from five to eight daily, plus an extra on Saturday. They increased traffic by an amazing 150 per cent, but lost money according to accounting figures. The 4-wheeled vehicles seating 46 passengers were built by AC Cars Ltd. Powered by a BUT 150hp diesel engine, they had a top speed of approximately 55mph. Apart from being cheaper to run than a steam train, each was manned by just a driver and ticket-selling conductor/guard, thus saving the cost of the booking office expenses at Tetbury station. Extra passengers were collected by re-opening Culkerton station, closed 5 March 1956, and building new, low-cost, rail-level halts at Church's Hill and Trouble House – the latter, the only halt in the country just serving an inn. Although the new service seemed profitable the branch closed to passengers 6 April 1964, having closed to freight 5 August 1963.

Culkerton 30 May 1956, view Up. The station closed to passengers 5 March 1956, reopened as an unstaffed halt 2 February 1959 and finally closed with the branch 6 April 1964. Author

Kemble to Cirencester

Cirencester was the original temporary terminus of the CGWUR, but with the extension to Gloucester on 12 May 1845, it became the terminus of the branch line from Kemble. At first Kemble station was unusual, being merely a platform for changing trains, as landowner Squire Gordon would not permit a public station with outside access to be built on his land.

It is interesting to note that CGWUR timetables stated that London time was about 7½ minutes before Cirencester time. It was the ease of travelling which the railways brought about which led to the adoption of Greenwich Mean Time throughout the country. The branch was converted to standard gauge 22-27 May 1872. Kemble station was fully open to the public 1 May 1882.

Like the Tetbury branch, railbus services began 2 February 1959 with 14 trains each way Mondays to Fridays, with two extra trains on Saturdays, while Sunday services remained unchanged at four in each direction. A new halt was opened at Chesterton Lane, while a further halt at Park Leaze opened 4 January 1960. Figures were most impressive: 130,000 passengers yearly – 2,500 a week, or an average of about 13 per train. Particularly on

The initial timetable for Cirencester trains. *Gloucester Journal* 5 January 1841.

Saturdays, the railbus was overcrowded, but replacement with a conventional diesel multiple-unit was not the answer, as for much of the time a railbus supplied an adequate capacity. A DMU would also have interfered with cyclic working in conjunction with the Tetbury branch.

Park Leaze Halt.
Lens of Sutton

The original intention was to run railbuses through to Swindon to obviate the tiresome change at Kemble, but this proved impossible as the lightweight vehicles could not be relied on to operate the signalling track circuits on the main line. Despite the apparent success, the passenger service was withdrawn on 6 April 1964 and freight on 4 October 1965. Two of the four AC Cars railbuses have been preserved.

Advertisement in
the *Wilts &
Gloucestershire
Standard* 1 January
1960.

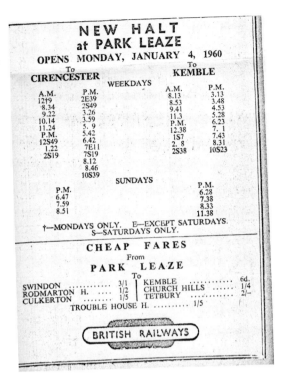

NEW HALT
at PARK LEAZE

OPENS MONDAY, JANUARY 4, 1960

To CIRENCESTER			To KEMBLE	
WEEKDAYS				
A.M.	P.M.		A.M.	P.M.
12†9	2E39		8.13	3.13
8.34	2S49		8.53	3.48
9.22	3.26		9.41	4.53
10.14	3.59		11.3	5.28
11.24	5. 9		P.M.	6.23
P.M.	5.42		12.38	7. 1
12S49	6.42		1S7	7.43
1.22	7E11		2. 8	8.31
2S19	7S19		2S38	10S23
	8.12			
	8.46			
	10S39			
SUNDAYS				
P.M.				P.M.
6.47				6.28
7.59				7.38
8.51				8.33
				11.38

†—MONDAYS ONLY. E—EXCEPT SATURDAYS.
S—SATURDAYS ONLY.

CHEAP FARES
From
PARK LEAZE
To

SWINDON	....	3/1	KEMBLE	....	6d.
RODMARTON H.	....	1/2	CHURCH HILLS	....	1/4
CULKERTON	....	1/5	TETBURY	....	2/-
	TROUBLE HOUSE H.	....	1/5		

BRITISH RAILWAYS

Cirencester station, designed by Brunel and R. P. Brereton, his residential assistant, is a good example of Victorian Gothic railway architecture carried out in stone. Originally built with a small overall roof, this train shed was removed in 1874, the standard platform canopy replacing it not giving the required balance and making the building appear too tall and narrow when viewed from the ends. In 1956 partial rebuilding took place, H. E.B. Cavanagh taking great care to maintain the original style. It is now a listed building.

Chesterton Lane
Halt. Lens of
Sutton

Cirencester station
in use as a bus
station, 30 July
1981. Author

15 **Significant Accidents**

ALTHOUGH GLOUCESTERSHIRE has had a number of serious railway accidents resulting in death and injury, thankfully only two were very serious and only one really catastrophic.

The first major accident in Gloucestershire provided an instance of the advantage of the broad gauge in a collision. About 10.00pm on 5 November 1868 an Up cattle special, the 1.30pm ex-Carmarthen, consisting of 26 cattle wagons and a brake third for the guard and accompanying drovers and hauled by 0-6-0 *Tantalus*, almost stalled west of Awre Junction. The time interval system of railway working was still in force. After a goods train passed, signals were set at Danger for eight minutes, then left for seven minutes at Caution before the signals were returned to Clear. The criticism of this system was that a train may have come to a halt before the next signal and the following train would have no warning.

Leaving Lydney 22 minutes behind this cattle train was Waverley class 4-4-0 *Rob Roy* hauling the Up Mail from Milford to Paddington comprising three coaches, brake van and a luggage van.

Due to a sharp curve the driver of *Rob Roy* only spotted the goods train's tail lamp only 120yd ahead, was unable to stop in time and crashed into its rear killing three drovers and injuring five other drovers and the guard. The youngest drover was aged thirteen. All were travelling in the brake-third. 39 cattle were killed. Such was the benefit of the broad gauge that no one in the passenger train was killed. *Rob Roy* was not seriously damaged only suffering a dented smoke box and buffers plus a broken tyre. The locomotive was repaired at a cost of about £50 and not withdrawn until February 1872. When Captain Tyler, the Board of Trade inspecting officer saw *Rob Roy* three days after the accident it was 'still smeared with the blood of the slaughtered cattle'.

Broad gauge 4-4-0 *Rob Roy* following the collision west of Awre Junction 5 November 1868. Dead cattle can be seen beside the track. Author's collection

4-4-0 *Rob Roy* on the crushed remains of the third class brake van. Author's collection

Regarding *Rob Roy* the *Gloucester Journal* reported: 'To the great strength of its material and build the engine-driver and fireman, and very probably the passengers, owe their lives. The comparatively little damage sustained by the engine is truly remarkable, considering that it was going at something like 35 miles an hour when it encountered the opposing body. Indeed it must, but for its ponderosity, have toppled over after mounting the trucks and crushing everything beneath it like matchwood. It settled down as it were into a cradle formed by the axles and splintered flooring of the trucks, thus bringing the train to a standstill...The escape with life of any of the men who were riding in the end carriage [of the cattle train], which was the first truck struck by the engine, is truly marvellous, and can only be accounted for in that the train was only going at the rate of something like eight miles an hour, up an incline, and the coupling-chains were consequently extended, so that at the moment of contact the extended condition of the train formed a kind of elastic reception to the attacking body, as truck after truck was forced home to its buffers.'

The drovers were hurled from their coach on to the embankment. The sheet iron roofs of the cattle trucks collapsed on the beasts trapping them. 'They were, it was found, so pressed and entangled together in some of the trucks that it was deemed expedient, as the only means of releasing the living stock, to place a rope round the horns of the dead beasts and drag them out by the sheer force of an engine.'

Driver James Turner of the Mail said that after the accident, for safety he shovelled the fire out and eased the valves to permit steam to escape. Driver Robert Seys of the cattle train, said that his train slowed to 8mph on the rising gradient of 1 in 316 and frosty rails. He knew of the accident by the noise and the surge of his engine when the couplings slackened.

The inquest jury travelled in a special train to the scene of the accident. The Coroner said that 'The most extraordinary part of the business was that the train was travelling too slowly to avoid destruction, and that it was going too fast to enable the guard to alight and put down detonators to prevent the catastrophe'. The Jury's verdict was 'accidental death' and they handed their fees to the guard's widow.

The second serious accident in Gloucestershire happened almost exactly sixty years later. It was an hour before sunrise on a still autumn morning of Saturday 13 October 1928. Signalman Harry Button was on duty in the signal box at Charfield. Following a telephone conversation with his control office at Fishponds, he decided to shunt the 9.15pm Wolverhampton to Bristol goods train in order not to delay the 10.00pm Leeds to Bristol mail train which was shortly due behind it. From his box Button watched GWR 2-6-0 No 6381 slowly start to back its 49 wagons and brake van into the refuge siding. While this was happening, in addition to the Down mail approaching Charfield, there was also the 4.45am Up empty freight from Westerleigh Sidings to Gloucester.

He pulled off the signals on the Up line for this empty freight to pass through, but left the three Down signals against the mail because, of course,

Steel underframes of the wooden coaches piled against the north side of the bridge at Charfield. GWR 2-6-0 No 6381 can be seen under the bridge. Author's collection

A steam crane lifts an LMS coach underframe. Lying on its side is the tender of GWR 2-6-0 No 6381. Author's collection

Damaged wagons beside Charfield goods shed. A steam crane is beyond. Author's collection

Damaged wagons beside Charfield goods shed. Author's collection

due to the safety device of mechanical and electrical interlocking, they could not be cleared until the Bristol-bound goods trains had completely reversed into the siding.

The Down mail passed the previous signal box at Berkeley Road Junction travelling at its normal speed of 60mph and Button, as he watched the goods backing, kept glancing at his track circuit indicator for the approach of the mail, wanting to change the points as soon as possible and pull off the signals in order not to delay it a moment longer than necessary.

GWR 2-6-0 No 6381 is below the bridge. Author's collection

A Class 3P 4-4-0 passes through following the accident. The northern side of the bridge is damaged and sheets cover smashed wagons. Author's collection

On 3 August 1981 the author's father contemplates the grave at Charfield where some of the victims are buried. Author.

Imagine Button's horror when he realised that the mail had failed to stop at his outer home signal! Simultaneously, the up empty freight passed through Charfield station. He knew that three trains were about to collide and he was powerless to prevent a catastrophe.

Class 3P 4-4-0 No 714 and its mail train grazed the last two wagons of the GWR train setting back into the siding and struck the right hand rear end of the locomotive tender of GWR No 6381. This resulted in No 714 being de-railed and coming into contact with the wagons of the passing Up empty freight and then ploughing to a standstill on its side. Its tender, together with the GWR engine became wedged below the overbridge and with the wreckage of the destroyed wagons, blocked the forward progress of the mail train coaches. This resulted in the first five vehicles of the mail piling themselves on each side of, but chiefly below the bridge in an inextricable mass of steelwork and timber, the momentum of the whole train being absorbed in the destruction of the first five vehicles. The wooden bodied coaches were lit by gas and so all the ingredients for a holocaust were present.

Fire started in the wreckage, rapidly grew into a furnace with the result that eventually the first seven vehicles of the mail, two loaded wagons on the Down goods and a number of empty wagons were burnt out.

Immediately after the collision, Harry Button informed the control office at Fishponds, Bristol that a serious accident had occurred and asked that ambulances and breakdown trains should be sent from Gloucester and Bristol.

Stationmaster Brown on his way to the station saw flames at the bridge and arranged for a chain of men with fire buckets to check the blaze on the station side of the bridge and also provided axes and bars to assist helpers in releasing some of the passengers. He telephoned Wotton under Edge police station, asking them to advise doctors, nurses and ambulances to be sent quickly, to summon assistance from brigades at Dursley, Stroud and Bristol and also to get in touch with the Bristol Royal Infirmary in order to prepare for cases. Some of the injured were sent to Berkeley Hospital.

An ambulance belonging to Messrs Lister & Co arrived from Dursley and a train with ambulance men and equipment from Bristol. Stretcher cases and other injured passengers were placed in this train. Meanwhile fire brigades had arrived and were at work. The Bristol brigade arrived in 35 minutes and pumped water from a stream 100yd distant. Despite everyone's labours, the blaze lasted for twelve hours. Out of a total of approximately 60 passengers travelling on the mail, 16 lost their lives and 24 suffered injury; in addition, 13 Post Office sorters, as well as the driver and fireman of the GWR goods and both guards of the LMS trains were hurt. Of the total of 41 wounded, 11 were taken to hospital and detained. Medical opinion on the bodies of the victims recovered from the wreckage was, as far as could be determined, that death was caused by multiple injuries received, and not from burning.

And the cause of the accident? Colonel J.W. Pringle, inspection officer for the Ministry of Transport said that he could not accept the accuracy of the statement of Driver Henry Aldington or Fireman Frank Want that they saw a green light at the distant signal. He therefore concluded: 'The responsibility for this collision rests upon Driver E. H. Aldington, who, in my opinion, passed the distant signal for Charfield in the warning position, and subsequently the outer and inner home signals at danger. To a minor extent, I think responsibility rests also upon Fireman F. C. Want.' Colonel Pringle recommended that Automatic Train Control be installed to prevent misreading of signals; that coaches be made stronger and the desirability of abolishing gas lighting.

At the inquest on 30 and 31 October, the coroner interpreted the jury's verdict as one of manslaughter and committed Driver Aldington for trial on that charge. He appeared before the local magistrates on 20 and 30 November. They found there was not a *prima facie* case and he was discharged. On 1 February 1929 at Gloucester Assizes, the jury returned a formal verdict of 'Not Guilty'.

This was a very proper decision for both men declared with convincing emphasis that, although they had admittedly failed to see the home signals, they saw the distant perfectly distinctly showing clear. Aldington said that owing to the misty conditions he had crossed the footplate and was standing behind his fireman peering ahead. They had both seen the green light about fifty yards away. Want immediately exclaimed "He's got it off, mate". After the collision in which he miraculously escaped serious injury, Driver Aldington helped in the rescue work until the fire made it hopeless.

The signal certainly could have shown green if a heavy object had been placed on the wire, or the wire deliberately pulled by someone between the signal box and the signal, but whether this did in fact happen, we shall probably never know.

There is one other strange feature about the accident. Two charred and unrecognizable bodies, possibly of children, were among the victims and their identity was never established. It seems incredible that two children should travel on a night express without someone being aware of the fact, yet nobody came forward to claim them, and they could not be connected with any of the other victims of the accident. They were buried in an unnamed grave in Charfield churchyard on the hill above the railway, together with those of ten other named victims.

16 **An Overview**

WHAT HAVE railways done for Gloucestershire? Before the coming of railways life in the county moved at a slow pace – even getting from one side of Gloucestershire to the other was impossible in a day except on the very few stage coach routes. For many, travel was unnecessary because they lived and worked within walking distance of their homes. Agriculture was mostly dairying, the climate favouring meadows and butter and cheese generally stayed fresh long enough to travel to market. Oats were important as horse feed for coaching inns. The introduction of railways caused a dramatic change to the lives of some innkeepers and farmers; innkeepers on once busy roads lost their trade, and farmers had to change to growing other crops.

Railways offered a greater variety of employment than had been available in the district before its arrival. To progress through the railway ranks one needed to move, no longer staying in the same house or even in the same native village. Sometimes only a day's notice was given to report to another station.

The coming of the railway led to a greater use of coal for cooking and heating than hitherto, for, until railways, transportation of coal had been expensive and wood was the alternative fuel. With rail transport available a greater variety of building material could be used, not just local stone or brick, but different materials brought cheaply from a distance such as slates and tiles which rendered thatch out of date.

With cheap and rapid transport milk, with its very short life, could be sent by rail to urban markets; a cloth mill could readily supply the whole country, rather than just the local district. The railway enabled the cottager's wife to travel to a larger market town where she could receive a better price for her butter, cheese and eggs, more than offsetting the cost of her ticket.

Railways affected diet: no longer did one have to rely on what was grown in one's garden or was grown locally. Food could be transported cheaply from, or to, other parts of the country. Cattle and sheep were sent from Gloucestershire and early potatoes and tomatoes brought in, while such things as bananas could be imported and distributed.

Railways enabled people to gain a broader understanding by travel. The Great Exhibition of 1851 could be reached by cheap excursion from Gloucestershire and that meant that many people visited the metropolis who would not have otherwise done so.

The Workmen's Early Morning Return enabled people to travel cheaply by rail as long as they reached their destination by 8.00am. This time limit was imposed to prevent white collar workers who were better paid and could afford a full price or season ticket, from taking advantage of cheap fares.

Railways played a vital part in the war effort in both World Wars, particularly affecting Gloucestershire when they carried troops, ammunition and other supplies to the south coast. Gloucestershire had a number of docks used for importing food and war material from overseas, its ports having the advantage that shipping could avoid the dangers of sailing through the English Channel.

How has passenger transport changed between the eighteen-forties and 2010? In the eighteen-forties, as today, not all Gloucestershire settlements were served by rail, and road transport was necessary for at least part of the journey. By the nineteen-hundreds many settlements were served by rail, a walk of up to two miles to a station being thought not unreasonable. In the early part of the twentieth century there was little alternative to rail travel, but today travel from one part of the county to the other is probably more conveniently done by road, unless other factors come into the equation such as crowded roads, parking problems or lack of driving ability. Because of the closure of local stations, short distance rail commuter traffic is less common than formerly, but in 2010 rail travel certainly comes into its own for long distances. Rail travel is more restful for the traveller and better for the environment.

One difference to rail traffic over the last twenty years is that excursion trains have all but disappeared. Another change is that today's trains are of fixed length and inflexible. Until about forty years ago, a sudden influx of traffic would produce one or several extra coaches or even a duplicate train. Today services are run with the minimum number of vehicles to maximise the investment and overcrowding can be a serious complaint. Rail freight has also changed. In the eighteen-forties railways were the common carrier and would transport any item from a small parcel to an elephant, or tons of coal. Today the railway only deals with bulk items such as stone from Tytherington. A freight train is almost a rare sight in 2010, yet in the nineteenth or twentieth century, lineside watchers would have seen as many freight as passenger trains.

And what of the future for the railways of Gloucestershire? Here the author might be permitted to indulge his personal vision. I would like to see more encouragement to use the train, rather than the car, for longer journeys. Free station parking would help, perhaps not in larger towns where people should be encouraged to use the bus to reach the station, but certainly at more rural stations. I would like to see plenty of space on trains, rather than passengers packed in airline style. Space is limited in a car and space could pull people from the car into the train. Why is it that an old age pensioner can travel free, say from Cheltenham to Gloucester by bus, yet has to pay to use the more environmentally-friendly train?

I don't anticipate many more stations being re-opened in Gloucestershire because each stop delays a train and if a train is slow people will not use it because it might be quicker to go by road, but I would like to see a new station at Gloucester on the north to south line. The Filton – Henbury – Avonmouth line could be re-opened to passenger traffic with stations at Henbury, Hallen and Chittening. If the mile of line between Tytherington and Thornbury was reopened, people from Thornbury could quickly reach Yate and Bristol by public transport and if the service was extended through to Portishead, platforms would not be blocked at Temple Meads by terminating trains. A Parkway station at Charfield would have the advantage of being close to the M5 and be convenient for Thornbury and Wotton under Edge. If, when the third Severn Bridge is built on the site of the former railway Severn Bridge, it carried a railway in addition to a road, it would offer a diversionary route when the Severn Tunnel is closed for maintenance.

At the time of writing, it is proposed to electrify the line from Badminton through the Severn Tunnel. The Association of Train Operating Companies propose an infill electrification including Kemble to Gloucester and Bristol to Birmingham. Were this to happen, all-electric Intercity Express Programme trains could be used between Cheltenham and Paddington, rather than the hybrid diesel/electric versions now being considered.

Largish urban areas such as Gloucester/Cheltenham and the Stroud Valley could use tram-trains with single trams converging on a centre and then formed into a train to reduce line occupancy through the centre and then uncoupled and sent on radiating lines the other side. Running could be along streets, through tunnels, or along redundant or active railways with spare paths.

And what of those railways closed and not brought back into use? A number of them, their formations almost forgotten except for use as unofficial footpaths, are now becoming official paths and cycle ways offering gentle routes through the heart of the countryside and hopefully away from the sound of road transport.

Suggested Further Reading

Anon *Midland Railway System Maps (The Distance Diagrams) Vol 4* (Peter Kay n.d.)

Anon *Midland Railway System Maps (The Gradient Diagrams) Vol 6* (Peter Kay 1999)

Ashworth, B, *The Last Days of Steam in Gloucestershire* (Amberley Publishing 2009)

Ashworth, B, *The Last Days of Steam in Gloucestershire, A Second Selection* (Alan Sutton 1990)

Barnsley, M, *Midland & South Western Junction Railway* (Wild Swan Vol 2 1991, Vol 3 1995)

Bartholomew, D M, *Midland & South Western Junction Railway, Vol 1* (Wild Swan 1982)

Bick, D, *Gloucester & Cheltenham Tramway and the Leckhampton Quarries Lines* (Oakwood Press 1987)

Bray, N, *The Cirencester Branch (*Oakwood Press 1998)

Body, R, *The Severn Tunnel* (BR WR & Avon Anglia 1986)

Christiansen, R, *A Regional History of the Railways of Great Britain Vol 13 Thames & Severn* (David & Charles 1981)

Clark, R H, *An Historical Survey of Selected Great Western Railway Stations Layouts and Illustrations* (Oxford Publishing Co Vol 1 1976,Vol 2 1979, Vol 3 1981)

Clinker, C R, *Register of Closed Passengers Stations and Goods Depots 1830-1977* (Avon Anglia 1978)

Cooke, R A, *Atlas of the Great Western Railway* (Wild Swan 1997)

Cooke, R A, *Track Layout Diagrams of the Great Western Railway, Section 19A Bristol* (Author 1992)

Cooke, R A, *Track Layout Diagrams of the Great Western Railway, Section 19B Avonmouth Lines* (Author 1996)

Cooke, R A, *Track Layout Diagrams of the Great Western Railway Section 20, Swindon & South Gloucestershire* (Author 1988)

Cooke, R A, *Track Layout Diagrams of the Great Western Railway Section 22 Midland & South Western Junction* (Author 1982)

Cooke, R A, *Track Layout Diagrams of the Great Western Railway Section 28 Worcester-Oxford and Branches* (Author 1997)

Cooke, R A, *Track Layout Diagrams Section 34 Birmingham to Cheltenham* (Author 1977)

Cooke, R A, *Track Layout Diagrams Section 35 Gloucester and Cheltenham* (Author 1978)

Cooke, R. A, *Track Layout Diagrams of the Great Western Railway Section 36 Ross, Monmouth and Chepstow* (Author 1985)

Cooke, R A, *Track Layout Diagrams of the GWR Section 37 Forest of Dean* (Author 1996)

Dale, P, *Gloucestershire's Lost Railways* (Stenlake Publishing 2002)

Handley, B M & Dingwall, R, *The Wye Valley Railway and the Coleford Branch* (Oakwood Press 1998)

Hateley, R, *Industrial Locomotives of South Western England* (Industrial Railway Society 1977)

Hateley, R, *Industrial Locomotives of Central Southern England* (Industrial Railway Society 1981)

Hemmings, W, Karau, P & Turner, C, *The Banbury & Cheltenham Railway* (Wild Swan 2004)

Household, H, *Gloucestershire Railways in the Twenties* (Alan Sutton 1984)

Huxley, R, *The Rise and Fall of the Severn Bridge Railway 1872 – 1970* (Amberley Publishing 2008)

Jenkins, S C, *The Witney & East Gloucestershire Railway (Fairford Branch)* (Oakwood Press 1985)

Karau, P, *Great Western Branch Line Termini* (Oxford Publishing Co 1977/8)

Long, P J & Awdry, A S, *The Birmingham & Gloucester Railway* (Alan Sutton 1987)

Macdermot, E T revised Clinker, C R, *History of the Great Western Railway* (Ian Allan 1964)

Maggs, C G, *Branch Lines of Gloucestershire* (Alan Sutton 1991)

Maggs, C G, *Bristol Railway Panorama* (Millstream Books 1990)

Maggs, C. G, *Railways of the Cotswolds* (Peter Nicholson 1981)

Maggs, C G, *The Birmingham Gloucester Line* (Line One Publishing 1986)

Maggs, C G, *The Honeybourne Line* (Line One Publishing 1985)

Maggs, C G, *Rail Centres: Bristol* (Ian Allan 1996)

Maggs, C G, *The Bristol and Gloucester Railway* (Oakwood Press 1992)

Maggs, C G, *The Mangotsfield to Bath Branch* (Oakwood Press 2005)

Maggs, C G, *The Midland & South Western Junction Railway* (David & Charles 1980)

Maggs, C G, *The Nailsworth & Stroud Branch* (Oakwood Press 2000)

Maggs, C G, *The Swindon to Gloucester Line* (Amberley Publishing 2009)

Maggs, C G, *The Yate to Thornbury Branch* (Oakwood Press 2002)

Mitchell, V & Smith, K, *Bath Green Park to Bristol* (Middleton Press 1999)

Mitchell, V & Smith, K, *Cheltenham to Andover* (Middleton Press 2000)

Mitchell, V & Smith, K, *Stratford upon Avon to Cheltenham* (Middleton Press 1998)

Mitchell, V & Smith,. K,. *Branch Lines Around Avonmouth (*Middleton Press 2004)

Mitchell, V & Smith, K, *Bromsgrove to Gloucester* (Middleton Press 2006)

Mitchell, V & Smith, K, *Gloucester to Bristol* (Middleton Press 2004)

Mitchell, V & Smith, K, *Swindon to Newport* (Middleton Press 2004)

Mitchell, V & Smith, K, *Swindon to Gloucester* (Middleton Press 2005)

Mitchell, V & Smith, K, *Gloucester to Cardiff* (Middleton Press 2005)

Mitchell, V & Smith, K, *Branch Lines Around Ross on Wye* (Middleton Press 2008)

Mitchell, V & Smith, K, *Branch Lines around Lydney* (Middleton Press 2008)

Mitchell, V & Smith, K, *Branch Line to Monmouth* (Middleton Press 2008)

Mitchell, V & Smith, K, *Banbury to Cheltenham* (Middleton Press 2009)

Mourton, S & Pixton B, *Birmingham to Bristol – Portrait of a famous Midland route Part 1 Birmingham to Cheltenham* (Runpast Publishing 1993)

Mourton, S, *Steam Routes around Cheltenham* (Runpast Publishing 1993)

Norris, J, *The Bristol & South Wales Union Railway* (Railway & Canal Historical Society 1985)

Oakley, M, *Gloucestershire Railway Stations* (Dovecot Press 2003)

Paar, H W, *The Severn & Wye Railway (A History of the Railways in the Forest of Dean Part 1)* (David & Charles 1963)

Paar H W, *The Great Western Railway in Dean (A History of the Railways in the Forest of Dean Part 2)* (David & Charles 1965)

Parkhouse, N & Pope, I, *Edwardian Dean in Colour* (Lightmoor Press 1995)

Pope, I, How, B and Karau, P, *The Severn & Wye Railway* (Wild Swan Vol 1 1983, Vol 2 1985, Vol 3 1987)

Postle, D, *From Ledbury to Gloucester by Rail* (Amber Graphics 1985)

Potts, C, *An Historical Survey of Selected Great Western Railway Stations Part 1* (Oxford Publishing Co 1985)

Randolph, S, *The Tetbury Branch* (Wild Swan 1985)

Robertson, K & Abbott, D, *GWR The Badminton Line* (Alan Sutton 1988)

Robertson, K, *Great Western Railway Halts* (Vol 1 Irwell Press 1990; Vol 2 KRB Publications 2002)

Russell, J H, *The Banbury & Cheltenham Railway 1887- 1962* (Oxford Publishing Co 1977)

Sands, T B, *The Midland & South Western Junction Railway* (Oakwood Press 1990)

Smith, P, *An Historical Survey of the Forest of Dean Railways, Layouts & Illustrations* (Oxford Publishing Co 1983)

Smith, P, *An Historical Survey of the Midland in Gloucestershire. Station Layouts and Illustrations* (Oxford Publishing Co 1985)

Smith, P, *The Dursley Branch* (Oakwood Press 1981)

Vincent, M, *Lines to Avonmouth* (Oxford Publishing Co 1979)

Walker, T A, *The Severn Tunnel* (Kingsmead Reprints 1969)